W9-CER-062

DATE DUE

COPING

AS

a Foster

Child

COPING AS

a Foster

Child

**Geraldine Molettiere Blomquist and
Paul B. Blomquist**

THE ROSEN PUBLISHING GROUP, INC/NEW YORK

Published in 1992 by The Rosen Publishing Group, Inc.
29 East 21st Street, New York, NY 10010

First Edition

Blomquist, Geraldine M. (Geraldine Molettiere)
    Coping as a foster child / G. M. Blomquist and Paul B. Blomquist
— 1st ed.
    p.   cm.
    Includes bibliographical references and index.
    Summary: A discussion of ways to make living with foster
parents and living in a foster home a better experience.
    ISBN 0-8239-1346-5
    1. Foster children—United States—Juvenile literature. [1. Foster
home care.] I. Blomquist, Paul B. II Title.
HV881.B58   1991
  362.7'33'0973—dc20
                                                    90-30594
                                                       CIP
                                                       A C

Manufactured in the United States of America

ABOUT THE AUTHORS ◊

G eraldine Molettiere Blomquist, a social worker for the past fifteen years, has worked in mental health clinics, schools, and protective services. Presently a therapist in therapeutic foster care for the Adams County Department of Social Services in Colorado, she develops long-term permanent plans for foster children, supervises and trains foster parents, and provides therapy to children and teens. She also served as a consultant to public schools and the YWCA.

A graduate of the University of Connecticut Graduate School of Social Work and of Bloomsburg State College in Pennsylvania, she was active in student affairs and political action groups advocating social change.

Married, with two daughters aged three and six, Geraldine Blomquist enjoys an active life-style with her family that includes biking, skiing, camping, and swimming. She is also an accomplished cook, the winner of numerous regional and national cooking contests.

Paul Blomquist is a science librarian with a double degree in mathematics and chemistry, much involved in the technical aspects of library work. He is highly proficient at on-line bibliographic retrieval and has also been involved in development of library software applications.

Contents

Introduction

Struggles between teenagers and their parents are fairly common, and are usually worked through, but occasionally the need for foster care arises. Also, for teens in families that have a history of poverty, violence, or abuse, the need for crisis intervention is urgent. For such teens, foster care is available.

Foster care is difficult for teens. Adults often can rely on their own emotional resources, which teens usually lack. Teens in foster care have the additional burden of being displaced from home, family, and friends.

In one year of foster care a teenager may be in three or more homes and as many schools. Forced to make new friends with each move, he or she may decide it is easier not to make friends at all. With no friends and with classmates who do not understand what foster care is like, he or she often feels that no one cares.

Life often seems unfair to the foster teen. He or she may have lost one or both parents either from death or abandonment; or the home may be so full of anger that the teen may not be able to live there any longer. Also, teens in foster care often are unable to see their brothers, sisters, or grandparents.

Although foster teens often feel hopeless about their future, they do have some control by the choices they make. This book explores many of the good and bad choices made by foster teens. It also discusses the care programs most often used by state or city departments of social services:

- Shelter homes, receiving homes, crisis centers
- Family foster homes, therapeutic foster homes
- Group homes
- Residential child-care facilities
- Emancipation programs
- Relative homes

These programs provide the assistance of caring adults—foster parents, social workers, counselors, and staff. Teens learn what it is like to be in a family that cares. Trained adults help the young person accept and express angry feelings in a positive manner and move on to a more rewarding life as a responsible adult.

CHAPTER 1

What Is Foster Care?

F or teens in a difficult home situation, the prospect of living elsewhere seems like a great idea. "If
I could only get away," they may think, "everything
would be all right."

Teens in abusive homes may run away or they may be
removed from the home by police or a social services
representative. Others may leave home to stay with friends
or relatives. For teens no longer able to live at home,
several placements are available.

Shelter Home, Receiving Home, Crisis Center

Sandra recalls the day she first went into a receiving home.
"It was my thirteenth birthday. On the way to school my
eleven-year-old sister told me that our stepfather was
molesting her. I was so upset I ran all the way to school,
and when I arrived I started a fistfight with the first person
I came upon." When Sandra's teacher began to question
her about her unusual behavior, Sandra became even more
upset. She ran to the bathroom, where she swallowed ten
aspirin tablets. Taken to the hospital emergency room,
Sandra confided to a psychiatric assistant that her step-

father had been molesting her as well as her sister. She was then placed in a receiving home.

"For the first time in years," Sandra recalls, "I truly felt safe from my stepfather." She stayed in the receiving home for several days while an investigation was conducted.

Like Sandra, many teens in crisis situations need foster care on short notice. Shelter homes, receiving homes, and crisis centers are designed for such emergencies.

These facilities are usually available for one day to two months until more suitable living arrangements can be made. Possibly located in a home, a church, or a school, the facility is supervised by a rotating staff twenty-four hours a day. A caseworker from the social services agency frequently visits the teen to discuss problems and to plan for future placement.

Teens in emergency care are expected to attend school. Some go to the nearest public school; others continue in their home school. Some facilities have a classroom and a teacher on the premises.

Foster Home

Since she was a toddler, Jennifer has lived with her grandmother. Now fourteen, she has become increasingly arrogant and assaultive at school as her grandmother's physical and mental health has deteriorated. Alerted to Jennifer's problems, the school social worker and the county caseworker made arrangements to move her into a foster home.

Jennifer remembers her feelings at the time. "At first I was fearful. I didn't know who these people were; they could have been madmen for all I knew. But after a few days I found they were good people. It felt so good to have someone take care of me after a year of taking care of myself, my brother, and my grandmother. My foster mom made me meals, made sure I looked well when I went to school, and cared about my schoolwork."

Some teens, like Jennifer, are placed in family homes that include the foster parents' own children as well as other foster children. They participate in family activities as they would if they were living with their own family. Most of them attend the neighborhood public school, but some may attend special schools that better meet their academic and emotional needs. A caseworker visits the teen and the foster parents frequently to discuss progress. In any type of foster care the social service retains legal custody of the teen.

Group Home

At fifteen Laude is known for being aggressive, carrying weapons, and using drugs. Although Laude has avoided serious criminal charges, he was recently charged with malicious trespass, breaking curfew, and shoplifting. Because he has a record of several such offenses, the court ordered him into a one-year mandatory out-of-home (meaning his parents' home) placement. Laude was placed in a group home.

A group home, usually located in a residential neighborhood, has a rotating staff to supervise the teens twenty-four hours a day. Sometimes a married couple live in the home, and other staff members provide services such as transportation, preparing meals, and shopping.

A social worker or counselor visits each teen to discuss problems, progress, and future plans. Most of the residents attend public school, but some group homes have classrooms for teens who cannot behave appropriately in school. The length of stay at a group home is usually three months to one year, occasionally longer.

Residential Child-Care Facility

Because Antonio, thirteen, has been in seven foster homes in the last three years with disappointing experiences, he no longer feels he can trust adults. Antonio blames all his disappointments on others. "None of this is my fault. At the last foster home, the father pushed me against the wall. At the home before that they locked me out of the house. And at the home before that, they wouldn't give me dinner." Although these foster parents may have taken actions more drastic than appropriate, Antonio takes no responsibility for his poor attitude, destructiveness, and verbal abuse. To protect him from hurting himself and others, the social worker placed him in a residential child-care facility (RCCF). Similar to a boarding school in a campus-like setting, the RCCF allows teens to live in cottages or dormitories, go to school, and have access to recreational facilities. Residents attend group therapy sessions and may also have individual therapy. Family members may also attend family sessions with the teens.

Emancipation Program

Rhonda has spent all of her adolescent years in foster care. Although she liked her most recent family, Rhonda wanted to be on her own. "I really enjoyed being with Dave and Renee. I liked being around their children, but I didn't want to live by their rules anymore. I'm seventeen now, and I want to be on my own. I know I seem young, but in a way I've been on my own for years. I've had to make decisions that teens who live with their families never have to make. I am afraid, but I'm ready."

Rhonda was placed in an independent living program, designed to assist older teens in going from foster care to living on their own. In an emancipation program teens living alone or with other teens in an apartment are assigned a caseworker who helps them learn to be independent and self-sufficient. They are usually required to go to school and sometimes to have a job as well. In return, a social service agency pays the teens for doing their job—that is, going to school and going to work. Payment, usually in the form of rent and food assistance, is gradually reduced as the teens learn to provide for themselves.

To succeed in this program, teens need to have some degree of maturity and to be responsible for their behavior. The program usually lasts from one to three months but may last up to one year.

Relative Home Placement

Although living with a relative is not typically considered a foster home placement, many teens are placed in this alternative living situation. Although supervision and financial assistance vary from state to state, such placements offer one clear advantage: The teens remain with a member of their family. Disruptions of their lives as well as feelings of alienation and distrust are less intense. Placements with relatives are most successful if the teen comes from a stable family. For families with many problems, a public program may be more appropriate.

How Is a Placement Chosen?

Someone other than the teen usually chooses the placement based on the family history and the teen's reaction to problems, adults, and peers. Some state laws require specific placements for teens like Laude. Availability of openings also plays a part. Finally, most placements are governed by age and sex guidelines and restrictions that limit the options.

CHAPTER 2

From Adoption to Foster Care

"Hi! I'm Rhonda. Next week I'll be eighteen. Then the state says I can be independent, which means I can live anywhere I want. It means no one will be watching what I do, no one will be telling me how to spend my money, and I won't have a curfew any more. When I was sixteen, that sounded really great, but now I'm scared.

"I've been in foster care for a long time. I first left my family when I was thirteen, and I've been through a lot since then. Sometimes I think foster care was good for me. I was a wild child, not wanting to listen to anyone; but other people—therapists and social workers—say I was given the shaft by my parents. I don't know if that is true or not."

Rhonda has many strengths, one being her desire to communicate to others. She also has a strong desire to maintain ties with people she has known. Although adopted as an infant, she had many problems in her early years. She always felt different from other children.

She had a learning disability, which was not detected until high school. Medical tests determined that neurological damage to Rhonda's brain caused her to have a minor perceptual problem. Although the problem was unnoticeable to most people including her teachers, it made reading and writing difficult for her. A bright child, she was able to manage in grade school, but in high school her inability to read at grade level became evident. No longer able to hide her disability, Rhonda became increasingly disruptive, distracting other children in class and manipulating some of them into breaking the rules. At home, Rhonda was also having problems. Her adoptive parents had separated when she was ten, and her mother—with whom she lived—did not understand her. The two argued continually.

"I remember my mother being mad at me a lot of the time. She didn't have any patience, and sometimes I was afraid she would hurt me. I remember that she did hit me a few times. I thought it was horrible then, but I've heard stories from others that were a lot worse.

"Back then small things seemed to be big deals. I guess Mom was under a lot of pressure. I didn't really know what was going on, but it seems like something could have been done for her. If someone could have taught my mother how to discipline me, I believe things might have been better."

Rhonda has put a lot of thought into what has happened to her. Many teens just react to the situations that they are forced to cope with, and Rhonda did that too. For years she reacted impulsively. Yet hard times have made her think and listen to others, and she sincerely wants other teens to learn from her mistakes. Rhonda has been able to use what counselors, foster parents, friends, and family have told her, but it wasn't like that at first.

"I remember when I first went into foster care," Rhonda recalls, "I was mad at my mom. When I ran away, I called the police and told them I wanted a foster home, but they took me to a receiving home. Eventually I was placed in a foster home, but I hated the family. They had locks on their refrigerator and cupboards, and they were always picking on me. In a few days I ran away again. This time I was sent to live with my dad.

"My father had remarried, and his wife, who was very young, didn't like me from the start. No one could discipline me, and I wouldn't listen to anyone. I started smoking cigarettes to make my father mad. Finally, I ran away. Running away had become a habit. Every time I thought someone would hurt me—physically or emotionally, mostly I thought they would reject me—I'd run away. Even now, going on eighteen, I still feel that way. Running away has been an easy way out for me because I know I can always find someone to help me. It got so that when I thought someone was going to discipline me I'd run away. Now that I look back, I know what I needed was discipline."

Rhonda is pretty hard on herself. What she really needed was caring people to nurture her with loving discipline. Fortunately, she was drawn to that type of person. Rhonda cared about others, and she cared what others thought about her. That quality made people want to care about her, which was extremely important. When teens allow others to care for them, people will try to help them grow in a positive manner.

Rhonda tried to develop an extended family of people who would take the time to listen to her and assist her in her personal growth. If took much searching to find people who would care for her, but she persisted. At one point Rhonda even wanted to find her biological family. She had the emotional strength or instinct to know that continuing contact with people is essential for positive development, that she needed people whom she could count on for the consistent message: "You're okay."

Children from traditional families find reassurance from their family members. They don't have to ask for it; it's just there. Many foster teens refer to children living in traditional families as being privileged. On the surface, they mean material things such as clothes and toys, but in reality they mean the free-flowing reassurance and positive messages that children deserve. Foster children are not so lucky. Their families are usually riddled with problems such as poverty, depression, and violence. Their parents are most often divorced. Often they don't even know where their fathers are. Such children have a hard time allowing others to help them.

Although it is difficult for a foster child to develop a strong self-concept, it is not impossible. Foster children, particularly adolescents, can develop positive relationships with others and learn to feel good about themselves.

When Rhonda was fifteen her adoptive mother gave her up. The social worker explained to Rhonda that her mother had signed a paper saying that she beat her daughter and that she no longer wanted to be her mother. Rhonda was crushed.

"The social worker told me that my mother could no longer control my behavior," Rhonda sadly remembers.

"She was afraid Mom would hurt me, so she counseled her to give me up."

However, Rhonda had some hope. She had been living in a foster home, and the mother had said she would like to adopt Rhonda. When Rhonda learned of her mother's relinquishment, she believed her foster parents would adopt her. Unfortunately, when she discussed it with her foster mother and the social worker, she was told that the foster father did not want to take on the financial and emotional responsibility of another child, particularly one entering the tumultuous teenage years. Rhonda, devastated, ran away, vowing never to care for anyone again.

"I never thought I could feel so betrayed," Rhonda recalls, "first by my mother and father and then by my foster family. I started hitchhiking, meaning to go as far away as possible. I started in Colorado and within three days I was in Florida. People were kind to me on the way. They gave me food and rides, and as I look back I realize how lucky I was that no one hurt me. When I got to Florida I was broke and alone, so I went to a mall hoping to meet some kids I could stay with. When the mall closed, I had found no one. I was beginning to get really scared when a security guard found me. That night I stayed in a detention cell at the youth prison, and the next day I was on a flight back to Colorado. In many ways I was relieved, because I knew I couldn't keep running. When I got back, I was sent to another foster home. This family seemed fairly nice, and they had other teens there who were nice to me. So once again I let my guard down and began to trust that someone might care."

Rhonda again has a special strength in allowing herself to trust adults. Unfortunately, this ability did not help her this time either. About a year later the foster parents decided they no longer wanted to care for foster children. Rhonda would have to move again. This time she was angry.

"When I received the news I was hurt; but instead of running away I started 'acting out,' as the social worker calls it. I started lying and stealing. One time I even hit my foster father. I told him I hated him and that he was a lousy father. I don't think I meant it, but I was hurt.

"I also had to change social workers. I liked Pam a lot, and I was really upset. I didn't want to change, but Pam said she would keep in touch, and as the years passed she did. At least once a year I hear from her, and we go to lunch together.

"When I moved into the new foster home I was angry," Rhonda remembers. "I didn't want to do anything they wanted me to do. The parents wanted to supervise me closely, but I hated that. I was now fifteen, and I knew how to take care of myself. Sometimes they would try to confront me with my problems, and I didn't want to hear it. One day I finally blew up. The foster mother didn't like the way I had my clothes in my drawer and threw them all out onto the floor. My mother used to do that to me. It reminded me of all the pain I had living with her. All the fears of being abandoned were just too much to handle. I pushed everyone out of the way and ran out the door. I hid at my boyfriend's parents' house for a few weeks. After I had calmed down, they notified the social worker where I was. This time the social worker made arrangements for me to go into a therapeutic foster home."

Therapeutic foster homes offer special care for children who have had an especially difficult life. The social workers have small caseloads so they can spend more time with each child. The children and teens receive individual therapy and sometimes group therapy. The foster parents are usually trained to handle extreme behavior problems.

Such a home was found for Rhonda. The foster family and she were a good match. The adults were in their late twenties, and although Rhonda knew they were her parent substitutes, she also related to them as peers. They had two young children, whom Rhonda enjoyed.

Rhonda learned a lot from watching these foster parents care for their own children. She recalls imitating them when she helped out with the children.

"I learned how it should be between parents and children," Rhonda reflects. "Sometimes I thought they spoiled their children with so much love, but maybe it should be that way. This family had their difficulties, but their problems never changed their love for their children. I watched how they disciplined the children, and I plan to use what I learned with my own children someday. I don't want to be as harsh as my parents were.

"Things went pretty well for six months or so. I was still having problems in school, but my social worker arranged to get me into an alternative high school. It was ideal for me. I started to learn and to enjoy school. I vowed to myself not to run away again, and I also decided to graduate from high school no matter what. No GED for me; I wanted to graduate. I was able to keep both of those vows, although several times I came close to breaking them.

"When I turned seventeen I started having trouble with curfews, and I started skipping classes and drinking. I cared a great deal about my foster family and I didn't want to hurt them, but I couldn't live under someone else's rules. I sneaked out at night a couple of times, but I didn't run away. I told my social worker about my feelings, and I talked to my foster mom. Lucky for me, they listened. I entered an independent living program in which I could live in my own apartment provided I continued school and worked. If I kept the contract, social services would help me financially until I was eighteen.

"That's where I've been for the last six months. Sometimes it's very hard. My boyfriend and I don't always get along. Sometimes we have horrible fights. Yet I feel I'm making it. I am working part time at the diner and going to school. But I am scared too. The program ends next month, and I don't know if I will be able to take care of myself.

"As I look back, though, I can see some positives in what I've been through. I've learned to be independent and make my own decisions. They may not always be right, but I know I can decide. I've also learned to make and keep commitments and to follow through on promises to myself.

"I know I made some bad choices, but I can't go back and change them. I don't even know if I would want to change them because they are a part of me. I do know, however, that I can make better choices for myself now and in the future."

MAJOR PROBLEMS FOR RHONDA

For Rhonda, the stressful events of her early life made it more difficult for her to cope during her teen years. Some of her problems are similar to those of many foster teens; others are not. In later chapters other problems are discussed. It is important for foster teens to understand that each teen has a different background and family history, and each will face different challenges.

Abandonment

Rhonda has been abandoned several times, the first time by her birth parents. Until she was fifteen, she had no idea why she was given up for adoption at birth. During stressful times she would imagine what her birth parents were like. She thought if they only knew what she was going through, they would come to help her. When she sometimes imagined that they really did know where she was, she felt unworthy of their love and thought they did not rescue her because she was bad.

Of course, none of that was true. Rhonda's adoption had been confidential. Her birth parents did not know where she was, and her adopted parents did not know who her birth parents were.

However, Rhonda's thoughts and feelings are common to many adopted teenagers. When in emotional pain, they often fantasize about being rescued by birth parents. Also, as adopted children near emancipation they frequently begin a search for their birth families. Laws governing access to birth records vary from state to state, but most states have groups organized to assist the adoptee in his search. Later, when the adoptee plans to marry, and at the birth of an adoptee's first child, the desire to learn about his or her heritage becomes of great concern.

When Rhonda's parents separated, her life was in chaos. As is often common in divorce, there was a great deal of conflict between the parents. The mother became very depressed, and Rhonda, feeling responsible, tried to pull her out of it. She was unsuccessful. Her mother, angry and unable to manage her own feelings, sent Rhonda to foster care.

As children often do, Rhonda felt responsible for her parents' divorce. She thought her problems in school and her disobedience were the reasons for it.

Later Rhonda was devastated by the news that her parents had given up their parental rights. She knew she could not live with either of them, but she never thought they would give up on her entirely. The pain was almost unbearable. For years she tried to find some way to run from it.

Fear of Being Hurt

Rhonda readily admits that she fears someone will hurt her feelings. She seems tough on the outside, but she knows it's just a front. As a young teen she refused to let anyone get close to her. She had what she called her "antenna." Whenever she suspected someone might reject her, criticize her, or even discipline her, she ran away before they could do so. Yet she always came back. By running she gained the emotional distance that allowed her to feel safe. Even now she continues to keep a distance from those who care about her.

Teens who have been in foster care for a long time are often more sensitive than their peers. Frequently they are teased by others who do not understand the hardships of living in foster care. They often find it hard to confide in their friends for fear of hearing hurtful comments.

Running Away

Rhonda readily admits that for her running away was the easiest and quickest way to avoid facing problems and handling relationships. Whenever there was a conflict in any relationship—parents, substitute parents, boyfriends, girlfriends, or teachers—her first thought was to leave. At sixteen, Rhonda vowed to herself not to run away from her foster home again, and she kept that commitment. However, that did not prevent her from running away in other ways. Rhonda always left a difficult situation unless forced to face it.

On one occasion, Rhonda recalls, she was very angry with her foster parents. Despite her counselor's questioning, she refused to talk about the problem. Instead she walked from room to room with her counselor following, trying to continue the discussion. Although this was both maddening and funny to Rhonda, she remembers secretly feeling good that someone cared enough to pursue her in trying to discuss her feelings. It was then that Rhonda started to trust her counselor. Afraid of her trust and of being hurt by it, Rhonda ran away to Florida; however, she returned after only a few days. Rhonda continues to struggle with the urge to run away when faced with problems, but she knows that talking about the problem is a better choice.

THINGS THAT HELP RHONDA

Goal-Setting

Rhonda set goals for herself. She had daily goals: She would not ditch classes. She would do her homework. She would be in at curfew. She would not drink.

She had monthly goals: She would attend her peer counseling group. She would talk with her foster parents. She would discuss problems with her social worker.

Rhonda also set long-range goals. She did not want to run away from foster care. She would graduate from high school.

Rhonda choose those goals herself, and she made a commitment to herself to accomplish them. With the help of good foster parents, counselors, and teachers who were flexible yet firm, Rhonda accomplished many of her goals.

The daily goals were the hardest. Rhonda frequently wanted to skip school or stay out late if she was having fun. When she was unable to make her goal, she—with the cooperation of the adults involved—would start over. Their confidence motivated her to continue to reach for her goals.

Journal Writing

Rhonda found it helpful to write about her thoughts and feelings. She kept two journals. In one she wrote of daily events in detail. In the other she wrote her thoughts and feelings about those events and anything she was thinking. Looking back, she believes the writing helped her sort out her thoughts. Also, she was better able to talk about her feelings after she had written them down.

Group Counseling

During Rhonda's stays in foster care, she had been in several peer group counseling programs. She really enjoyed the groups and wished she had the opportunity to be in one continuously. She recalls one group that consisted of six children with an adult counselor supervising and structuring the sessions. Rhonda enjoyed the opportunity "to tell the others off without getting beaten up." How did she feel when others told her what they thought of her? "Sometimes I felt bad, but it was worth it just to have the opportunity to say what I really felt."

Individual Counseling

Rhonda, like many teens, considered counseling an intrusion on her privacy. Teens are intensely aware of what other teens think of them. Foster teens are already labeled as different, and many feel that seeing a social worker further marks them. Some fear that a counselor will discover their thoughts about themselves and others, which they already feel are too horrible to mention.

Rhonda wanted to feel she had her life in control. She wanted to believe she was beyond counseling, that she could take care of herself. Secretly, however, Rhonda enjoyed counseling. She liked having someone take her out for a soda and ask her what she thought. Rhonda felt that her counselors helped her devise some good solutions to her problems.

In the last few months Rhonda has not seen a counselor. Soon she will be on her own. She misses the attention she received and feels sad about losing it. Rhonda has had a number of counselors in her life, and she has kept in touch with several of them. This contact has given her a sense of continuity in her life.

Positive Self-Talk

Teens generally tend to feel negative about themselves. They are critical of how they look, how they sound, and how they act. They often underestimate their positive qualities and exaggerate their negative qualities. Foster teens are even more susceptible to this.

Foster teens need to look at their strengths. They need

to find the positive qualities in their parents and see those qualities in themselves. Otherwise they will view themselves and their families as losers.

One thing foster teens can do is talk to themselves about the positive aspects of their lives. For example:

Teen: (looking in the mirror) "I like the color of my eyes. They are the same color as my mom's. People always said she had pretty eyes."

Or they can remember the good qualities that parents and foster parents have pointed out.

Teen: (thinking out loud) "Mom always told me I had a knack of making people laugh. You know, she was right about that."

Revisiting Places and People

By the time Rhonda was fifteen, she had been in three foster homes and two group homes. In each placement she had made a significant attachment to some foster parent, counselor, or resident. When Rhonda expressed a desire to contact some of these friends of the past, her caseworker helped her find them. Nearly all were receptive to seeing her. Meeting the people who had nurtured her in the past gave Rhonda a knowledge of her own history and helped her feel better about herself.

SUMMARY

For several years Rhonda did not enjoy herself. She wanted to go to parties and dances and just go out with her friends, but she was never in one place long enough to develop solid friendships.

Once Rhonda had decided not to run away, she was able to invest herself in choosing friends who would not lead her into trouble and to involve herself in her foster family's life. She also used her counseling sessions to help her grow emotionally.

Rhonda didn't solve all her problems. She will continue to work on many issues throughout her life, but she has learned to develop support systems for herself and to seek out community resources to help her.

As she prepared to go out on her own, she had one more thing to say, "I wish someone had taught me how to cook."

CHAPTER 3

From Foster Care
to Adoption

BRIAN

For most of his seventeen years Brian has been in and out of nine foster homes, including his aunt's and his grandmother's. Although his foster parents adopted him last year, Brian still feels like a foster child who at any time may have to move. He is struggling to maintain his connection to his new family as he tries to grow into an independent and self-sufficient adult.

"Though I had lived there three years before they adopted me, I still feel different. Maybe I'm afraid that one day they will say, 'You can't live here any more,' like other foster parents. In a way I feel closer to my friends than to my new parents."

Katherine, his mother, who was an alcoholic and a drug user, married Tim at Brian's conception, but Tim was not Brian's father. During one of Katherine's drinking episodes she had met another man, and Brian was conceived that evening; she never saw the man again. Katherine eventually divorced Tim, and in later years she brought home many new boyfriends. She was a very poor parent, unable to provide for her five children either emotionally or physically. Frequently she left them alone while she went out drinking, and often she would be away for days or weeks, leaving them with friends, relatives, or whoever was willing to take them.

As a child Brian assumed that his life with his mother was normal, but as he got older he started asking himself, "What's going on?" His mother used the homes of friends and relatives as well as foster homes as a revolving door for her children. They never knew where they would sleep that night, and if they were at home they never knew who would be in bed with their mother.

"I remember we could do whatever we liked. There was never any adult telling us what to do. We lived in a mobile home for a while, and my older brother and sisters were always skipping school. I was five then, and we would go door to door asking for meals."

All this took a toll. "When I was in kindergarten I would fight with anyone. If someone looked at me the wrong way, I'd hit him. My mother thought it would be a good idea to teach me a lesson. She and her boyfriend made my brother, who was seven, beat me up so I would know how others felt. They made him keep hitting me until I had two black eyes. I didn't have the kind of childhood most kids have, like going camping and to baseball games with their dad. Heck, my father was a one-night stand and didn't even know I existed. I never knew what having fun was."

Many teens who grow up in foster homes describe similar feelings. Often if they remember a good or fun time it becomes tangled with a bad memory. That is true of Brian.

"I remember at six I almost killed a kid. This kid hit a friend of mine and called us names, so we started throwing rocks at him. I hit him smack in the middle of his forehead, blood everywhere. It really scared me because I thought I had killed him. To this day, I wonder about him. My mother locked me in a closet for three days. I just stayed there, afraid of what her boyfriend would do to me.

"After that we moved far away, to the coast. We found another mobile home, and we weren't there for more than an hour when Mom and her boyfriend decided to go to the beach by themselves. They were supposed to come back in an hour or so, but the next morning they still hadn't returned. A neighbor called social services, and off we went to a foster home. I never saw my mom again."

For Brian this was a turning point. He had grown used to on-again off-again care by his mother, and even at eight he had become self-reliant. He knew how to get food, and he could get himself off to school. He also made most of his own decisions. For Brian, adjustment to a foster home was very difficult. He was not used to adults making good decisions for him, feeding him, and making sure he was clean and properly clothed. He liked it and hated it at the same time.

Brian was angry at his mother for destroying not only his life but the lives of his brother and three sisters. The longer he was in the foster home, the angrier he became and the less he could understand how his mother could have done what she did. Because Brian kept all his feelings in, his anger came out in indirect ways like lying and fighting with foster siblings. Fighting was the only way he knew to get along, yet he remembers really liking his foster family and never wanting to hurt anyone. Fortunately, Brian had an outlet in sports. He was a talented baseball player, and he dreamed of someday being a professional.

Brian really enjoyed his first foster family. He liked the family activities such as camping and going to Disneyland. Yet just as he began to feel he belonged and think that maybe he could love someone, the bomb dropped—it was time to move! Brian's foster parents felt they could no longer handle his behavior and asked to have him moved. Although they liked him, they could not give him the kind of care he needed.

Brian remembers that the hurt was like all the hurts he had ever felt combined. "It was indescribable. It was overwhelming. You know, I could accept my mother's moving me around. Maybe I just put up with some of her faults. I was mad at her, but I don't remember feeling the kind of hurt I felt when the Bakers told me I was leaving. I think it was because I did like them. But they couldn't keep me, and that made me feel worthless and bad. I could handle it when my mom left me, but when a good home got rid of me I just couldn't handle it."

Although the move was traumatic for Brian, the new agency tried to lessen the shock by some "preplacement" visits. But for Brian the memory is a blur. "I don't think anything could have made the move easier. One day I was with the Bakers, the next day I was with the Tremolos. The Tremolos made a special effort to keep in touch with the Bakers, and I still see them now and then, but the hurt is always there.

"I thought I'd be with the Tremolos for a few months, but a few months turned into a few years. Yet even after I was adopted, I mentally had my bags packed. It's been nearly eight years now and I still wonder deep down when they'll get tired of my stunts and ask me to leave."

GENE

Gene, fifteen, has been in foster care for ten years in five different homes. Recently his foster parents adopted him, but like Brian, Gene still feels like a foster child who may have to move someday. Both boys struggle not only to maintain their connection with their new family but to grow into independent and self-sufficient adults.

Not sure why he still feels like a foster child, Gene reflects, "I think it's because my foster parents—I mean my parents—still have other foster children in our home. I think if they left I would feel better."

The other foster children consider Gene lucky, or "privileged" as one teen put it. And Gene *is* lucky to have found a home where the "fit" was good enough to let hearts and minds open and allow a teenager into the family permanently. Gene had that special something that made his new family love him in spite of the problems he had when he arrived, but he doesn't think luck had much to do with it.

"It was hard work! I had to make many compromises. My new dad always pushed me to the limit. You know, I was never one to talk about my problems, but he had some kind of radar. He knew when something was on my mind, and he would get right in my face, I mean nose to nose, and not back off until I talked. I hated it when he did that, but also I knew he was bugging me because he cared. He could get me to talk about my feelings as no shrink ever did. I'm not sure why, but I think it's because he never gave up on me. He made me feel like his real son. When he asked me a question about my feelings he wouldn't let me say 'I don't know.' Instead, he'd keep plugging until my feelings came out. You know, he made me feel important. I can't ever remember feeling that way before I lived here.

"Because my new parents, Sam and Helen, and their birth son, Steven, made me feel that they wanted me around, I tried to work on my behavior. It was a lot different from when I was with my birth mom. With her I felt like an animal. I know I will always defend her, but I also know I really felt hurt when I was with her. Sam and Helen allowed me to feel pleased with myself instead of hurt."

Gene's adoptive parents are exceptional. They have good intuition, and they also help teens identify their feelings. Foster teens often find it hard to sort out their feelings. Sometimes they are mad at their birth family and take it out on their foster family. Gene, for instance, had an incident with a younger foster child, Cindy. This girl liked to provoke the others, and she was particularly skilled at enraging Gene. At one point, he was so mad at Cindy that he started yelling, "It's not fair, Angel, you always get your way." Angel, Gene's younger birth sister, still lived with their mother. The foster parents, trained in psychology, seized the opportunity to help reconstruct his relations with his sister, and Gene talked to them about his feelings and fears. That is often a hard step for foster teens, and it was only possible for Gene because of the trust he had developed in his new parents.

Sensitive, caring, and skilled foster parents are hard to find. Many teens are so angry that they don't allow the foster parents to help them improve their life situation and their future.

PROBLEM AREAS

Both Gene and Brian have come a long way since they first entered foster care. The road has been difficult, and the road ahead will continue to be rocky. Both boys have had to learn to handle what might be called the ultimate rejection: being abandoned by their mother. Both remember vividly the last time they saw their mother as well as their respective father and stepfather. Both still carry hurt feelings, but they have gone beyond those feelings and have come to care about another set of parents. They have had to leave their birth family and make room in their lives and hearts for a new family. That is not an easy task. The scars of their hurts will always be with them, making their path difficult. For such teens life can be very frustrating; they may feel that just as they get one step ahead, something goes wrong and they fall two steps behind.

Angry Feelings

Both Gene and Brian have many feelings about their parents' abandonment, and both have had difficulty handling those feelings in a healthy and productive manner. Both received individual counseling and did not find it helpful. They felt it was intrusive and that a person had a right to keep his feelings to himself. Gene and Brian also felt that they could deal with their problems without help, yet both had foster/adoptive parents skilled in helping teens with special needs. That was fortunate for them, as they needed someone to intervene and help them direct their anger appropriately. Gene, holding back his true feelings, would at times feel overwhelmed and take out his frustrations by trying to bully others. "Sometimes when I'm angry, it makes me feel good if I can get someone else upset too," he says. "I know I shouldn't do that, but I do it anyway."

Brian, on the other hand, withdrew into himself when he felt overwhelmed and wouldn't tell anyone how he felt.

After withdrawing, he would sometimes—like Gene—try to get someone else upset. He recalls, "Once when I wouldn't talk to anyone and I was feeling mad, I called my foster sister on the phone and threatened to destroy her most prized possession." Although Brian learned to be more direct with some feelings as he got older, he still cannot talk about those feelings that hurt the deepest, holding them in check by denying and lying to himself and others. "I don't like to depend on anyone for anything, especially someone helping me. That is, I don't want to owe anyone any favors. If I talk to them, let my guard down, and they help me, I feel I owe them something. So I would rather not talk to anyone."

Because Brian chooses not to talk about his feelings, he at times becomes very depressed. "There was a time about a year ago that I wished I were dead. I didn't really think about how I would kill myself. I don't think I could ever go through with something like that, but I thought about what it would be like if I were dead. I imagined my funeral, who was there, and what they—my family and friends—would say about me. It was a terrifying, lonely time, but I did get past it."

Testing Foster or Adoptive Parent Love

Both Gene and Brian's parents continued to be foster parents after they adopted the boys. Gene has made it clear to his parents that he does not want other foster children in their home. "They want a lot of attention, and they get it. I want the attention. Other kids, especially little ones, get in your stuff. They're pests, and I want to punch them. Sometimes I do, and I get heck. So it would be better for me if they didn't live here at all." Gene has made this an issue to the point that his parents are considering no longer being foster parents. He has done other things to test their love. "Sometimes when I'm told to fix something, I pretend I don't know how. If they show me they pass my test; if they don't they fail. Then later I usually blow up at something else."

When he is mad, Gene also tries to hurt them. "When they won't let me do something I want to do, I'll say, 'You like the foster children better than you do me,' but they never pay attention to that one."

Brian also has tried to test his adoptive parents' love. He recalls, "They used to go on camping vacations. I hated to go with them because I always felt left out. My brothers (adoptive parents' birth children) were always talking about the fun of previous camping trips. I didn't remember having any fun at all when I was a kid, and I really felt out of place when I went camping with them. One year I complained so much about going that my parents arranged for me to stay with friends. I had a good time with my friends, but I really did feel bad that they left me. I said to myself, 'See, they don't love me like their real sons.'"

Lying and Stealing

Both Gene and Brian have had problems with this. Gene describes feeling bad about having the problem, yet when he talks about it he doesn't sound too regretful. "I steal money when I see it or when I want something I can't have. I know stealing is wrong, but I keep hoping that I won't get caught. I usually am caught, and then the consequences are hard."

Brian says, "Sometimes it seems like stealing and lying is just a part of me. I know it's wrong, but when I'm in a difficult situation I just do it without thinking. Sometimes I do it for no good reason at all."

Both teens know right from wrong most of the time, but when they are under pressure they choose do something they know is wrong. For many teens in foster care, this irrational behavior is brought on by a feeling of chronic emptiness. Brian described the feeling: "I felt like my body was full of holes, and I would try anything to fill them. In the heat of the moment, taking something I wanted seemed like a way to fill those holes. On days when I feel good about myself the holes seem smaller. When things go badly and I feel lonely, the holes seem bigger."

Low Self-Esteem

Teenagers sometimes have trouble feeling good about themselves. Many studies conclude that a high percentage express a desire to change their physical appearance. They think they are too short, too tall, too fat, or too thin, or their nose is too big, or they have funny hair. Gene and Brian have those insecurities in addition to feelings of worthlessness created by their abandonment. Self-identity comes from the feedback a person receives from others, and for foster teens that feedback has not always been positive. They often describe themselves as bad, the result of a life of emotional scarring from abandonment or abuse. They frequently regard themselves with the same distaste they feel their birth parents had for them.

School Problems

Like many teens in foster care, Gene and Brian have had difficulty with their grades. Yet many experts view education as a way to break the cycle of abuse and abandonment in which Gene and Brian will surely participate unless they can begin to feel successful. Both presently live in adoptive families that place a high priority on education and support them in their efforts.

In elementary school both Gene and Brian spent time in special education classes, and both worked hard to be placed in regular classes to escape the undeserved stigma of special education. Although proud of their accomplishments, both are still behind in academic skills and on occasion have to attend summer school. Yet with their parents' support the boys continue to plug away, hoping to finish high school and to obtain further academic or vocational training.

THINGS THAT HELPED GENE AND BRIAN
Sticking with My True Feelings

Brian said, "When I was younger I had trouble knowing what my true feelings were. I knew I was mad at something, but I didn't know what. I usually took it out on myself and sometimes on others. Now I realize that I should think about things. When I have that gnawing feeling in the pit of my stomach, I try to stop and think about what's going on.

"It also seems to help to review my life. I think about where I might be if I had lived with my birth mother all this time. My brothers and sisters still do, and every one of them has spent time in jail. The more I think, the more I understand myself. But I don't care too much for individual therapy. I believe everyone has a right to his personal thoughts. My therapist made me say things I didn't want to say, like, 'I hate my mother.' I did sort of hate her, but I didn't want to say it to anyone. But therapy did teach me what I could do so I didn't take so much out on myself."

Gene, too, doesn't like to talk about his feelings in individual therapy, and it is hard for him to sort out what they really are. "I know I need to talk about my feelings, but I don't like to. But I'm beginning to learn to talk about a problem before it gets big—I should after all these years."

Gene now frequently writes his feelings down. His parents provided him with a list of positive and negative feelings to help him identify his own. The following is a list similar to Gene's:

Positive and Negative Feeling Words

Positive		Negative	
Alert	Happy	Afraid	Guilty
Alive	Hopeful	Angry	Hateful
Amazed	Interested	Annoyed	Helpless
Busy	Joyful	Anxious	Hurt
Calm	Loving	Bad	Lonely
Comfortable	Peaceful	Bitten	Mad
Concerned	Proud	Bored	Mean
Curious	Quiet	Concerned	Nervous
Eager	Relieved	Confused	Sad
Elated	Secure	Depressed	Sorry
Excited	Surprised	Disappointed	Unhappy
Friendly	Trusting	Discouraged	Upset
Glad	Warm	Disliked	Worried
Good		Embarrassed	
		Frightened	

Write down the words that describe the way you are feeling. Write a sentence about what is making you feel that way. Then share it with a person you trust who can respond to you in an emphatic manner.

Write the feelings in a special notebook. Call it, "Book of Feelings." Use this book daily to record things that have happened to you. Record things that others said or did to you, what you did, and how you felt about it. Then record what you did or said that day, why you did it, and how you did it, and how you feel about it. Reread what you wrote each week. You should begin to see how your feelings make you behave.

Increasing Self-Esteem

It takes work for teens in foster care to feel good about themselves. Brian thought a lot about how he could improve his life. What he needed to work on was how he felt about himself. Rather than blaming himself, Brian needed to look at the positive, strong, and good parts of himself. Here are some exercises that helped Brian feel better about himself.

SELF-ESTEEM EXERCISES

1. Make a list of words that describe you. Circle the positive descriptions and think about them as part of you.
2. What messages have you recived while growing up? Circle the positive messages. How can you change the negative messages?
3. Are you different from five years ago? Of course, you are. You have grown up in many ways. List the many ways.
4. You will continue to change. What would you like to be like five years from now? Think about this seriously. What can you do now to help make it happen? Would a good education help? Would vocational training help? There are people who can help you accomplish your goals. List the people who can help you.

5. What do you like about yourself? List your strengths, accomplishments, and what others might like to know about you.
6. List the things that could help you improve your attitude. Use the suggestions below to help you maintain a positive attitude.

Your attitude about yourself is very important for good self-esteem.

- Your attitude is the way you think. If you think good things about yourself, you will feel better about who you are and where you are going.
- Your attitude is like a magnet. "Good attracts good."
- Your attitude could be the most important thing about you.
- With a positive attitude, you can do what you set out to do.
- Enthusiasm is a great attitude.
- A good attitude can and will lead to success.
- Your attitude can determine the direction your life takes.
- Believe you can do it.
- Try again and again.

7. List the kinds of things could make you feel happier? What can you do to make them happen? Is there anyone who can help you accomplish your goals?

Sports

Brian found sports to be an effective outlet in managing the stressful aspects of his life.

"When I was young I learned that I was talented in

athletics. I started out in baseball and did well. It made me feel good to be encouraged and praised by coaches, friends, and family. When I moved in with my foster/ adoptive family, all the kids played soccer. I didn't want to give up baseball, but I wanted to be like everyone else so I started playing soccer too. As it turned out, I became good at it, so good that I went to the state championships. Because of sports, I kept my grades up so I could keep on playing. I also met my best friends through soccer. I hope some day I can play pro."

Although many foster teens can do well in sports, many do not have the talent or motivation that Brian has. Some who are unable to get along with other students have difficulty playing team sports. Some do not have the opportunity, and some do not have the physical ability. Also, as teens get into high school, competition becomes keen for spots on a team. That was true for Gene. Somewhat overweight, he could not compete at a level needed in high school sports. Gene began swimming on his own. He found it reduced stress, helped control his weight, and allowed him time to think. Last summer Gene was excited to get a job as an assistant to a swimming teacher.

Spirituality and Hope

"There were some days when all I had was hope," Brian remembers as he recalls the events of his life. "If you don't have hope, you don't have much. When things were bad I would say to myself, 'I know I'll be all right.' I thought that no matter how bad it was, the sun would rise tomorrow; tomorrow would be a better day and things couldn't get worse. I also had a basic belief in God. I felt He was watching over me and would help me. When I was younger I would have never said that for fear someone would make fun of me. I had hope and faith that I was alive for some reason, and that kept me going."

Upon entering adolescence, many teens no longer want to be involved in religious organizations. Yet for some foster teens, religious organizations of any denomination can be sources of support. Church groups can fill the empty holes and provide a framework for moral development. For some, involvement in a church community helps sustain the hope that teens need to get though difficult times.

CHAPTER 4

The Waiting

Foster Teen

D aniel, thirteen, came to Bob and Sara's home after being released from a psychiatric hospital, where he had spent sixty days after a suicide attempt. It had been his second hospitalization in less than a year. Two years earlier, after his mother had died in a house explosion, Daniel had lived with several relatives, finally ending up at the home of his grandmother and step-grandfather. During the last year Daniel became very depressed, and his behavior at home and school became unmanageable, including breaking things and shouting obscenities. Frequently he threatened suicide, and he actively tried to hurt himself by sticking himself with pins, drawing rough tattoos on his arms, and playing chicken with cars. On the second anniversary of his mother's death Daniel attempted to cut his wrists. His grandparents tried to control him by hitting him with switches or threatening him with other punishments. Often they scared him with threats or accusations of being crazy. After the school nurse found bruises on Daniel, he was taken into the custody of social services and immediately admitted to a psychiatric hospital.

The hospital staff treated Daniel's grandparents and two sisters—who remained with the grandparents—in family therapy, and eventually they made enough progress for Daniel to be returned to their home. Several weeks later he returned to the hospital after having swallowed bleach, and it was decided that he could not return to his grandparents.

Since Daniel's mother was deceased and his father could not be found, the county department of social services placed Daniel in a foster home. The purpose was first to stabilize his emotions as he lived in a family setting, and second to teach him more effective ways of handling his feelings. A plan was to be developed for a permanent placement with the possibility of adoption. This foster home was to be his "practice family," a place for him to learn how to live in a family again and to prepare him for an adoptive family. Daniel needed to learn how an emotionally healthy family acts and how his negative behavior affects others.

Daniel's move into the foster home required adjustment. He had moved many times before, but it was always with a relative. In the foster home, not knowing anyone, Daniel felt alone and scared. Things were not going well for his sisters either. His older sister had run away to other relatives, and after bruises were found on the younger sister, she too was placed in foster care far from where Daniel lived.

Daniel recalls, "My greatest worry was for my sisters and particularly my younger one. Everything seemed out of my control. I was very mad, but I didn't know how to show it in the right way or I was afraid to. I either yelled at anyone who looked at me cross-eyed, or I sat in a corner and moped. Now I know I was just afraid something would happen and there would be nothing I could do about it."

The foster family, knowing how much Daniel wanted to keep in touch with his younger sister, made an effort to have them get together on special occasions.

"It was hard for me to accept," Daniel recalls, "but I had to let others be responsible for her; I had to take care of myself."

Daniel's grandparents wanted to stay involved in his life, but he refused to see them. Yet the decision made him feel lonely. He again become depressed and remembers thinking, "I don't have any hope: My mother is dead, my father doesn't want me, my older sister ran away, my other sister is far away, and I hate my grandparents—my whole family is falling apart. No one wants me and no one needs me."

When Daniel told his foster parents his thoughts, they put him on twenty-four-hour suicide watch with the help of his therapist. Daniel gave way again to suicidal feelings, but now someone was with him all the way helping him learn to face his feelings and finally to handle them. Yet before he could handle them, he cried, he shouted, and he broke things.

Daniel recalls how he panicked, "I think I went kind of berserk. I started breaking my own things, and then I broke other people's things. I even broke the patio door by putting my foot through it. My foster parents called the police. They put me in handcuffs and wanted to take me to the hospital, but my foster parents wanted to see me through. They explained what I needed to do and what they could do for me. If I could get control of myself, they would help me with my feelings. To my surprise, I did. I

calmed down and started talking about my fears. Then I
started crying as I recalled how I missed my mother. I felt
it was my fault that I couldn't keep her from dying. My
therapist explained that I was afraid to admit I was mad at
my mom for leaving me. Mom left us all in a big mess with
no place to go. I tried to say I hated her for it, but I
couldn't. I never knew how mad I was at her, but the
therapist and the foster parents helped me understand that
I could love her and miss her and still be mad at her. It was
a surprise to me that I could be mad at someone who was
dead. Admitting that was a turning point for me."

Realizing that his foster parents had exceptional
qualities, Daniel recalls, "I never knew anyone who took
the time with me that they did. They never gave up." As
he began to feel close to them, Daniel wanted his foster
parents to adopt him. Unfortunately, that is not possible. A
family has to be found willing to care for him until he is of
age. Many steps—rules, regulations, and evaluations—
must be gone through, yet Daniel's strengths will help him
find a permanent family. Smart and thoughtful of others,
Daniel also has a sense of right and wrong and of what it
takes to be accepted by others. Daniel has a lot to offer a
family.

A family for Daniel will need special qualities such as
patience and the ability to understand his depressions and
help him through them safely. A parent who panics at
Daniel's thoughts of suicide will not help him. He needs to
be handled carefully, yet confidently.

Daniel can still stay with this foster family for another
year, if necessary. If a permanent family is not found,
however, he must move to another foster home. That
would be traumatic for a teen as sensitive as Daniel. He is
very frightened as he thinks about it, "I don't want to move
from here except to an adoptive home. I like it here. I

know the family, and I know the rules. It would be hard to get to know someone else."

Daniel began the process of letting prospective adoptive parents know he is available by having his picture taken. The picture, placed in a directory, was circulated nationwide. Although Daniel would rather stay in his hometown, that may not be possible. There are many more special-needs children like Daniel than there are families wanting to adopt. Eventually most children are "matched" with a family, but sometimes the wait is years, not days or weeks.

Daniel was also seen on national television during a telethon. The interview was videotaped and sent to families attracted to Daniel. Daniel also attended an "adoption party" set up by the state agency, which brought together families interested in adoption and teens needing to be matched with a family.

Daniel went to all the interviews. "It was very hard. I didn't know who I was talking to, and I felt I was trying to sell myself instead of being myself. Sometimes it was fun when I got to meet television personalities and see myself on TV, but when it was over I felt sad. I thought no one would like me. The waiting was awful. I called my social worker every day to see if anyone had asked about me. After two weeks she told me there had been nearly 30 calls. She said I was a handsome guy on TV. I thought I looked pretty good, but I didn't know that good."

When Daniel came into foster care, he was angry with himself and his parents. He had to make many changes to survive, and he worked very hard at learning to feel better about himself. "I realized that I was all I really had, at least for right now. It may not seem like a lot, but it was enough. I had memories of loving times when my sister and I lived with my mom. It helped to think about them. For a long time I didn't want to care about anyone. Now I want to be part of a family again. My foster family is nice, and I would like to stay with them, but since I can't I want my own family. I want to have the same name as my parents. It seems all the hard work has paid off. Now a few families are interested in me. It makes me feel kind of good!

"The social worker screened the interested families and told them about me. There were also some things I wanted in a family. I want to be an only child if possible. I know from experience in this foster home that little kids take up a lot of the parents' time. It seems I always get into it with little kids. I'd rather not be around them. I also want a family that can spend a lot of time with me. Maybe part of me is still a little kid who wants all the attention. I want parents who want to talk to me and do things with me. Sometimes I think maybe it would be better to have only a dad. Mothers have let me down. My mother died, neither of my grandmothers could care for me. Maybe a single dad could do better."

Daniel's ideas about the kind of parents he wants are important in the selection of a family. Daniel has some favorite activities. He loves music, and like many teens he has favorite performers. He also takes pride in his ability to dance the latest steps, which he practices hour after hour. "I hope my new parents like music, or at least don't mind my listening to it. Music means so much to me. The words of many songs make me think of my life. If people kept me from listening to music, I don't think I could live with them.

"I also want parents who care about how I look. I like to look well when I go to school. In foster care you get used clothes or inexpensive styles. Someday I would like a pair of designer jeans. Other kids' clothes never really look right on me."

Daniel may seem too concerned with material things,

but most foster teens want things. In part, they want to be like other kids, but also things can be a substitute for what they really want—someone to care about them. Daniel, like most teens, wants to be liked by the kids at school. He also wants a parent who cares about him and a parent he can care about. As a child who lost his parents and then was shuffled about, Daniel was deprived of many things that children usually receive from their parents. To him, possessions make up for things he never had.

Daniel wants to be important to someone. He thinks that if his new parents buy him things, it will mean that they like him and will cover up his feelings of emptiness. It won't. Eventually, even after he finds a new family, he will have to face the feelings of loss that will always be with him.

Daniel's story seems to have a happy ending, or at least the beginning of a new story. A single father, Tony, has been found for him. Though Tony lives far away, Daniel is thrilled.

After several months of psychological testing and counseling for Tony, legal arrangements were made between the two states involved, and Daniel and his prospective father finally met. Tony thinks Daniel could be the son he always wanted. Tony's own father died several years ago, and he misses the relationship. Tony visited Daniel for a weekend, and they had a good time together. Later Daniel stayed with Tony for several weeks. Things went well, and it looks like a place for him. Times will be tough in the future. Daniel and Tony must adjust to each other, but they will have help. The adoption agency has skilled counselors to help them through the difficult first year; then they will be on their own. Challenges will still exist for both of them, but they have a good start and the prognosis is good.

PROBLEMS FOR DANIEL

Grieving

Although Daniel lost his mother three years ago, he never fully grieved or faced all his feelings about her death. Only nine when she died, he was moved from home to home and then was physically abused. He spent all his emotional and physical energy in just surviving. However, important feelings cannot be kept down forever. Sad to say, the longer one waits to face feelings, the harder it is and the more disastrous the impact. For Daniel these feelings eventually overwhelmed him and he exploded—he attempted to kill himself. His stay in the hospital helped; however, when he returned to his grandparents they tried to put another lid on his feelings. Daniel exploded again and was placed in a foster home. Frightened as he went into foster care, Daniel felt that the real world had not supported him as he needed. Luckily, Daniel's foster parents would not put a lid on important feelings and saw him through the difficult times. Daniel eventually faced his painful feelings and experienced the pain and anger; mastering his feelings allowed him to move past them and feel hopeful about his future.

Feelings of Hopelessness

After leaving his grandparents' home, Daniel panicked, feeling that he had nowhere to go. He felt trapped and all alone. When the boy went into foster care, his social worker talked with him about his fears. She explained that her job was to protect him and to find him a safe, permanent home. Daniel wanted to believe her. "I remember wishing that what she said was true, but I didn't really believe she could find me a place to stay."

The feeling of hopelessness is common for foster teens who make frequent moves and are never sure they have a home. Daniel felt it even more keenly because he was truly alone. Often expressed by fear, depression, physical illnesses, and suicide attempts, hopelessness can lead to helplessness. As foster teens feel there is no way out, that the future looks bleak, they often react dramatically.

Daniel tested those he lived with, and the foster parents passed the test. Gradually he came to believe that he was lovable, capable of giving love, and that a family could be found for him.

Anger

On first entering the foster home, Daniel frequently had angry outbursts. He threw things, shouted foul words, and tore up his room. Once he broke every light bulb in the basement. Another time he put his fist through a wall, resulting in a broken hand. Daniel seemed to get angrier with his foster mom than with his foster dad. He would talk and listen to his dad but ignore his mom. Once he would have hit her had the foster dad not intervened. For months his anger seemed out of control. Finally, on the anniversary of his mother's death he blew up. He realized that besides missing her, he was angry with her. To this day, Daniel is prone to temper outbursts, but the violence has stopped.

Physical Abuse

Daniel's grandfather did not know how to help him with the feelings that caused his temper outbursts. In trying to teach him to control his anger, the grandfather beat him, leaving welts and bruises all over the boy's body. For a while Daniel accepted the abuse, knowing no way out, but his bad feelings about himself worsened every day. Finally he attempted suicide, having learned that if he threatened to hurt himself severely enough, someone would pay attention.

In the hospital Daniel learned other ways of getting help. He learned to talk to trustworthy adults such as a teacher, social worker, clergyman, or nurse. It sounds easy enough, but when Daniel was being abused it never occurred to him to tell someone. He did not realize he had the power to do something. His grandmother, unable to protect him, just left the room when the beatings started. Then she made him wear long-sleeved shirts and long pants to hide the bruises. Daniel knew that if he told someone about the beatings he would be forced to leave his grandparents' home, and he had nowhere else to go. He didn't know it was against the law to leave bruises on children. He didn't know there were places for him to go. He didn't know that he had the power to change what was happening to him. It is important to know that no child needs to live with adults who hurt him.

THINGS THAT HELPED DANIEL

Skilled Foster Parents

When asked what helped him most, Daniel replied, "My foster parents—they listened to me and talked with me." Skilled foster parents are often hard to come by. Although teens don't control what home they go to, they can choose to be receptive to the skills their foster family may have. Every foster family has something to offer, something a teen can learn. Most parents care about their foster children and want to help them through the difficult situations they face. Foster fathers may be professionally successful or be athletic or have a rewarding hobby; as they share their lives with teens they enrich the sense of self-esteem. Some families have strong, confident mothers or kind, nurturing mothers from whom the foster teen can learn. Some families are good at allowing a teen a certain amount of independence. Other families have biological children who can become good friends and role models for the foster teen. Some foster families may seem to be in it for the money, but raising a foster teen is a tough job, and the money is not really very much. People who provide foster care do it because they care about teens and their future. Teens need to open up, allowing the foster families to care for them. In return for their care, some foster parents want something back—they want the teen's respect. Yet they know that caring about others is hard for young people with many problems. Foster parents don't want "undying devotion." They want to see the foster teen trying, growing, having empathy for others, and reaching goals.

Concerned Teacher

Daniel felt that he learned a great deal from his sixth-grade teacher, once a foster teen himself, who remembered how difficult life was for him growing up. He entered teaching hoping to help young people. When this teacher learned that Daniel was in foster care, he told Daniel about his life and promised to help him get through the sixth grade and foster care. He was sometimes tough, but whenever Daniel got behind in school work the teacher spent extra time with him. Sometimes Daniel got angry at the teacher, but he remained one of Daniel's greatest supporters.

Many people want to help teens growing up. Teens need to allow responsible adults to help them, although it is hard for many whose parents have disappointed them.

Grief Work

Daniel had very little opportunity to complete the grief process that is necessary for everyone after a significant loss. A period of mourning after a loss is necessary for people to move on with their lives. Our society prides itself on doing things instantly, yet we have not evolved to deal with emotions instantly. We can use a calculator to add numbers instantly or a computer to recall things immediately, but our emotional life needs time to make sense of our feelings. Resolution of grief feelings takes time.

The period of mourning differs for every person and every relationship. For a significant relationship such as a parent, the period of mourning or feeling pain usually lasts a year or so. For some it may be less, and for many it is longer, particularly if survival becomes paramount as in Daniel's case. If people do not reach some level of acceptance of the loss, the grief can disrupt any portion of their lives. In Daniel's case, the loss of his mother was sudden and unexpected, and his absence made him feel responsible. Other teens experience other kinds of loss.

Initially, Daniel put his mourning aside to handle the more pressing issues of survival. Eventually the biological and psychological necessity to mourn caught up with him, and ultimately he attempted suicide. Many grieving young adults become defiant and angry as a way of denying their pain, but if their loss is not addressed they can also feel helpless and hopeless. Daniel had well-meaning relatives who tried to cheer him up, not allowing him to examine his sadness and his anger. He recalls, "I thought it wasn't okay to feel sad. I remember the first Christmas after my mother died. I missed her so much. So did my sister. My aunt kept trying to make us feel happy about the holiday. We had to smile for pictures. When I look at those pictures now, I just cringe.

"After a while I started to use my sadness. I learned how to make people feel sorry for me. Later, I realized that I used the sad trick to avoid looking at how mad I was at my mom."

It is often hard for people to be honest about their anger at loved ones who have died. Daniel, feeling disloyal to his mom for being angry at her death, also felt guilty. These feelings make people uncomfortable, and some go to great lengths to avoid them. Daniel avoided thinking about his anger at his mom, and it came out onto others around him in sometimes surprising ways. Once he could talk about and accept his anger his outbursts subsided.

Grieving is a process of painful yearning that one needs to experience, admit, and share with others. It also involves letting go, a little at a time, the wish that the lost person return.

Teens usually need the help of a knowledgeable adult, a person willing to share the pain. Daniel needed a therapist, as his loss was complicated by many other psychological problems.

Anniversary Dates

People tend to observe the anniversaries of significant events—birthdays, weddings. In the same way we remember a significant loss or traumatic event each year, although we may not always be aware of it. Daniel, for instance, was unaware of his anniversary dates, but he needed hospitalization for his depression and suicide attempts on the anniversary of his mother's death and of his being sent to an abusive home. Shortly before those dates he became unreasonably angry and disruptive, followed by severe depression.

"I never realized there was a connection between my feeling bad and my losses," Daniel recalls. "I thought there was something wrong with me. Now I understand there were feelings I needed to face."

Being aware of anniversary dates helps one to prepare for unreasonable feelings and behavior and to exercise some control.

Managing Angry Feelings

Daniel had reasons to be angry. Eventually he learned that it was okay to be angry, but not to hurt others. "I didn't want to hurt others or break things, but once I got going whatever was in my way was my target. It was as if I had to destroy everything around me."

Anger can be used destructively or constructively. Sometime the person must make a choice about how to handle anger. Daniel recalls, "I was scared to say I was mad at my mom for leaving; I had to hide it, disguise it, or pretend I was out of control. Once I realized I no longer had to do that, it was a great relief." By then Daniel had developed bad habits in expressing his anger; he had to learn new ways.

Four steps are involved in the management of anger:

1. Awareness
2. Responsibility
3. What Can I Do?
4. If All Else Fails

Awareness. Daniel's first step, awareness and validation of his feelings, was the hardest because he had spent several years avoiding his feelings. Many teens cling to their anger; others may not even realize they are angry. Some may cover up their anger by depression or act it out by hurting others. Some, like Daniel, take out their anger on themselves.

What are the clues that can alert the teen to angry feelings? They may not always be the same. An angry teen may say, "It's not fair," or "You should . . ." Or the teen may say "Why can't I . . .," or "I always have to . . .," or even "I hate you." Instead of speaking, the teen may act out his anger by slamming doors, driving fast, running away, or sulking. Understanding the clues to angry feelings helps teens to understand and control their emotional life.

Responsibility. Once aware of anger, the foster teen needs to acknowledge it and take responsibility for the decisions growing out of it. "It's not my fault" is a common statement in disclaiming responsibility for angry actions. It is important to acknowledge these tenets:

1. I do not have control over another person's behavior. I only have control over mine.
2. Is my angry action helping me to get what I want or making it more difficult?
3. What can I do to help myself manage and cope with my anger?

What Can I Do? Many teens think, "You made me mad, now you make it right," but that kind of thinking usually leads to further frustration and anger. Teens can manage their anger in healthy ways by controlling impulses to act out, by thinking before acting, and by taking actions that are constructive rather than destructive.

Each angry person has control over what he thinks and can either hold onto the anger or find ways to lessen it. One can lessen anger by finding its true cause and communicating it to an understanding adult.

For example: "I am mad at my (birth) mother for not picking me up for our visit and for not calling and letting me know she wasn't coming. I am thinking angry thoughts about her when my stupid foster brother walks by. I would rather trip him and make him scream than think about how hurt I am by my mother's not showing."

Here are some things a foster teen might think about before acting impulsively:

1. I could trip him, avoid thinking, and make my foster mom mad at me for tripping him.
2. I could face my hurt and think about what I will tell her the next time I talk to her.
3. I can talk to someone like my foster parents about my hurt and anger instead of acting it out.
4. I can think about the possibility of a misunderstanding with my mother and check it out with her. Of course, she's done this before so I doubt there has been a misunderstanding.
5. I can think of ways to let my mother know that her actions have hurt me.
6. I can think of what else I can do with the free time.

Which of these alternatives is best? Some foster teens choose number 1 because it's the easiest, but other choices may be healthier, allowing the teen to look at thoughts and feelings and keep anger under control.

If All Else Fails. If all else fails foster teens can ask

themselves questions that a helping person would ask:
1. What would I really like to have happen here?
2. What do I really want?
3. What have I been doing to get what I want?
4. Does what I do work for me? Do I have what I really want?
5. I'm smart. Can I figure a better way of handling things?
6. Do I even want to?
7. How can I move my life in the direction I want?

Take time to think!

If angry foster teens still cannot move past the immediate anger, they may ask the following questions:

1. Why am I holding on to my anger?
2. What need does it meet?
3. Do I want someone to pay attention to me?
4. If so, is there a better way to get their attention?
5. Am I trying to gain control over someone with my anger?
6. Can I get the control I want with healthy behavior?
7. Am I hiding other feelings by having an angry outburst?
8. Am I hurt or disappointed?
9. Do I feel guilty or powerless?
10. Is this behavior getting across the message I want?

Keeping a journal of responses to these questions may also help foster teens learn to understand and control their anger.

CHAPTER 5

I Don't Want
to Stay Here

Now fourteen years old, Cody began his foster care experience five years ago. Before his parents' rights were terminated by the courts, Cody had been in six foster homes. Since he became a legally freed child one year ago, he has been in an adoptive home, seven shelter care facilities, one psychiatric hospital, and two residential child-care facilities. Cody ran away from many of these placements including the last, and it is now unknown where he is.

An angry child, Cody became more angry as he grew into a teenager. Unable to control his destructive behavior, he often broke personal possessions of friends, neighbors, and foster siblings. Cody never received a gift that he did not break or lose. He argued with anyone on any subject. If you said the moon was white; he insisted it was yellow. It was as if his life depended on his being right. Cody felt nothing was ever his fault; he refused to take responsibility for his actions. Around younger children he always ended up provoking, teasing, and hurting them; with kids his own age there was always an argument or a fistfight. After his adoptive placement was disrupted he was furious and vowed to take his anger out on everyone around him.

Cody thought he was angry at his adoptive parents for giving up on him, but deep down he was really mad at his birth mother for deceiving him. He had thought she cared about him, but when the judge and the social worker asked her to do things to get him back, she didn't do them. If Cody sensed that the family he was staying with was going to ask to have him moved, instead of waiting for the ax to fall, Cody would run away. He easily gained sympathy from strangers with stories about why he was alone on the streets. Sometimes he got weeks of food, housing, and clothing from a new family before they threatened to turn him in to the authorities. Then he would run away again to find somebody else to take him in.

Cody never knew his father. His maternal grandmother claimed that he was a wealthy man. She and his aunt frequently told him they were trying to find his father. Unfortunately, both women were mentally ill and nothing of what they said was true. Even when social workers told Cody that his father would never come for him, the boy continued to believe that someday he would be rescued. Cody's father was probably never aware of Cody's existence. His mother, whose history included prostitution, probably met him in the course of business.

Cody's mother was an alcoholic and a drug user as well. Her marriage several years ago did not improve her ability to care for Cody. The stepfather, also an alcoholic, physically abused the boy.

Frequently left alone while his mother and stepfather went out drinking, Cody knew how to take care of himself. He remembers as far back as kindergarten having to fend for himself. "I remember doing whatever I pleased. Maybe I should have been scared, but I wasn't. I could go where I wanted and do what I wanted and nobody could stop me." When school started, Cody had a difficult time. "I thought I could still do anything I wanted, but I couldn't. They put me in time-out every day. I would scream and they would call my mom at the bar to come and get me. It used to be my trick to get her out of the bar and away from my stepdad. I got pretty good at it. It was sometimes the only way I could see her. She would pick me up, beat my behind, and take me back to the bar with her, my stepfather, and my little brother."

Cody's mother couldn't control him at home either, but she also could not control herself. "After one of her worse drinking binges, she came home and beat my back raw with a lamp cord because I had let the dog outside loose. I was only eight and a half. The next day the school nurse saw the marks and reported it to social services, and they took me to foster care."

For the next several years Cody was in and out of foster care as his mother tried to follow case plans approved by the courts to get him back. Cody's behavior continued to be unmanageable, and foster homes couldn't keep him. His mother kept promising to do better, but never did. She would promise to visit him, then not show up or even call. "I remember waiting at the window looking at the clock and wondering if she'd show up. I'd pace back and forth. My foster parents said I looked like a caged panther. After an hour or two I'd give up, knowing she had let me down again, but I would never admit it. I always made some excuse to try to fool myself."

After his mother disappointed him, Cody would not tell anyone how hurt and mad he was. Instead, he would get into trouble, usually hitting another child or breaking someone's toys. He always denied he felt any pain.

The times he got to visit his mother were not much better. She had a small place without even a bed for Cody. She always made a big deal about her plans to get a bed, but she never did. "I thought that was a sign that she didn't really want me there anyway," said Cody.

Cody never knew what to expect of her. "Some days she would drive up to the foster home unexpectedly, say hi, and want me to go with her. Of course, I didn't have permission to go. Sometimes she would call me every day or two or three times a day, and then I wouldn't hear from her for a month. Sometimes I hated her, and other times I missed her so much. She always called me her "All-American Boy." I don't know what that meant, but it was supposed to be something nice and caring. I took whatever kind of caring I could get from her, even though I didn't understand it."

His mother's inconsistent behavior is the biggest contributor to Cody's present problems. Her empty promises were not meant to hurt Cody, yet they did. They gave him false hope about being able to return to his mother's home. In turn, Cody reacted to other people the same way. He too made promises he couldn't keep. He insisted that his behavior was okay and that everyone else was wrong. The inconsistency of his upbringing will impact Cody for his entire life, affecting his relationships in work, play, and love. It will characterize his relationships with parent figures, girlfriends, and spouse (probably more than one can be expected). When someone does not learn consistency in childhood, it is very difficult to be consistent in adult life. Having friends takes being a good and consistent friend. Doing well in school and work takes persistence and consistent effort.

Cody's mother's parental rights were eventually taken

away by the courts. She was unable to follow through on any plan established to get him back. One would think that would be the end of it, and Cody could finally move on. Not so. Cody's family refused to say good-bye. They continued to give him false hope that he would return to them, and they continued to blame other people for their problems. Although Cody never saw his mother again—the courts would not allow it—he did have occasional visits with other relatives. Although older children and young teens in foster care commonly have contact with some family members, at least until they are adopted, this was disastrous for Cody. Instead of giving him permission to move on and wishing him a good future, his family allowed Cody to cling to the false hope that he would return to them. To make matters worse, his mother sent messages of false hope through the relatives.

Cody eventually was placed in an adoptive home far from his birth family, but the adoption was doomed to fail. He continued to talk to relatives by phone and receive letters from them. Within six months his behavior was so intolerable that the adoptive father asked to have him removed. Cody liked his adoptive dad, despite all his internal conflicts, and had begun to trust him. This frightened Cody. He didn't think it would last, so he proved it by acting out until the adoptive father gave up.

Cody recalls, "I really like my dad. He was a great guy, but how could a great guy like me? I knew if I trusted him, he'd leave, so I did everything I could to keep him away so that when I had to leave it wouldn't hurt so bad. But it didn't matter. When it came time to leave, it still hurt. I'm really mad at him for giving up on me; he was my only hope."

Cody has serious problems with which psychological therapy has not been able to help him. He needs intensive and extensive specialized therapy to help him sort out his feelings. After the failed adoption, Cody was sent to a residential institution that had the kind of help he needed. Sadly, however, Cody didn't want any more help. He, too, had had enough. "I don't want to talk to anyone; I don't want to be in foster care; I don't want to be here; I don't want to be adopted again. I can take care of myself, and that's what I'm going to do!"

Sure enough, Cody left during the night. Several days later, dirty and hungry, he was picked up by the police. When placed in a shelter, Cody said, "I'm still not staying!" He kept running away and being picked up. Once the social worker even resorted to sending him to a family member. Cody lasted there several months, but that too did not work out. He was then placed in a group home. Winter had come and Cody was not quite so willing to run, but as luck would have it, the home was shut down because of a cut in funding. Faced with the prospect of moving again, Cody was off and running. He got better at hiding out, and the social worker got tired of searching. Whenever he was picked up and placed somewhere, he ran away the next day.

When Cody turned sixteen he asked the court to emancipate him. This was unusual, but since social services could not provide for him or protect him, the judge allowed it. Cody could live on his own as long as he stayed out of trouble with the law.

Prospects for Cody are not good. He is one who fell through the cracks. People cared for Cody, but no one knew how to reach him and help him turn his life around. I wish I could say there was a happy ending to the story, but there is not. Cody is still on the run. Soon he will be eighteen. He has been abused severely, and that will catch up with him. He may eventually abuse a child. He may engage in a series of lesser offenses like shoplifting and eventually be caught and sent to prison. Or he may become a mass murderer or serial killer. It is unknown. The best services society had to offer were provided, but they were not enough.

PROBLEMS FOR CODY

Lack of Trust

Teens who experience many changes in living situations and many disappointments from people they care about have little reason to trust anyone. They learn to reject others before being rejected. Cody frequently said, "I can't count on anyone but myself."

These negative feelings and subsequent behaviors serve to keep people at a distance. The fragile psyche of a Cody protects itself by not allowing anyone to get close enough to hurt. Also, teens like Cody often interpret discipline as dislike rather than as guidance toward appropriate behavior. Thus discipline often makes them feel worse about themselves, reducing further their already low self-esteem. Feeling attacked, they have an even harder time trusting, so they cope either by running away or by demonstrating negative behavior that keeps others away. For Cody, this pattern of not trusting and running away was impossible to break.

Inability to Say Good-bye to Birth Family

Even after the courts revoked his parents' rights, Cody never fully separated from his birth family. They continued to give him false hope that they would rescue him. Cody needed permission from his family to move on and have a good life without them. His mother was too self-centered to handle the idea of allowing her son to have a healthy attachment to someone else. Her inability to say good-bye to Cody sabotaged the boy's future.

Lack of Sincerity

Sometimes Cody seemed phony or less than sincere. Because he did not have a strong sense of self, he did not know how to act with other people. Responsible adults not only tried to model appropriate behavior to Cody but also pointed out inappropriate and phony behavior. Cody just learned to be a better actor. The older he got, the more skilled he became at manipulating others. Cody said "I love you" quickly to people he barely knew, softening them up to get what he wanted. He probably didn't even know he was doing it. He just knew it worked.

THINGS THAT COULD HAVE HELPED

Cody could have been helped had he been able to look at himself, his behavior, his attitude, and his past. He could still find help, but he would have to want to. Change for Cody would be no easy task.

Individual Counseling

Cody has always thought that therapists didn't know much. He didn't like what they had to say because he didn't want to look at himself.

Individual counseling by a professional could help Cody separate his feelings about his birth family, his foster family, his adoptive family, and his friends. In therapy, he could examine the problems created by his behavior and his negative attitude. Cody needs to realize that the decisions he makes should be those of a mature adult. He could find help at a community mental health center. These centers, which usually provide a sliding fee scale for persons with limited incomes, have experience helping adults like Cody. However, he has to be the one to take action.

Accepting Responsibility

Cody does not see the world as others do. Rather he distorts his view of the world to the way he wishes it was. To thrive as an adult, he will eventually have to take a good look at his actions and their effect on others. Keeping a journal has helped some teens to understand their behavior. Writing sometimes makes a problem more real. For example, if a teacher unjustly accused a teen of cheating on a test, most would simply deny it. On the other hand, a teen like Cody might get into a large argument and disrupt the entire class. For such teens it would be helpful to write in a journal not only what happened word for word but also all their thoughts and feelings. In time, reviewing the confrontation as it occurred will put the incident in perspective. The teen can then better internalize the event and accept responsibility for his actions.

Building Relationships

To grow into a healthy productive adult, Cody needs to learn to develop healthy relationships. Because of his life experiences, Cody may find he is attracted to persons who can get him into trouble. Relationships need to be examined and avoided if they prove destructive. This will be especially hard for someone like Cody who does not have many friends; yet groups are springing up in many cities that can help. Adult Children of Alcoholics, Adults Who Were Physically Abused as Children, Teens and Adults Who Were Sexually Abused as Children are just a few. Such groups, which usually accept teens, are listed either in the telephone book or in the weekend sections of the local newspaper. Classes for people with difficult childhoods are offered in many community adult education classes, and churches may have groups available. Community mental health services, hospital outpatient services, and private therapists also may provide such groups.

Changes for Cody will be difficult; learning to make good choices for oneself is harder than it sounds. Teens in foster care can learn how to make good choices from a trustworthy person such as a foster parent or a therapist. For a teen on his own it is much harder.

CHAPTER 6

From Here to There

and Back Again

J
ose, seventeen, is the son of a Hispanic and a Native
American. He has spent the last six years in and out of
shelter homes, foster homes, group homes, and a
drug/alcohol treatment center. Everyone in his family,
including himself, agrees that Jose's problems began when
his parents separated and eventually divorced. In reality,
however, his problems began much earlier and merely
surfaced at the time of the separation.

Eleven when his parents separated, Jose became
obviously upset and started hanging out with older kids,
skipping school, staying out late, drinking, and smoking
marijuana. Says Jose, "I wanted my parents to know I was
mad at them, disappointed and hurt that they split up. I
had seen my friends' families split up, and I thought mine
was different."

Before the separation Jose's parents had lived together
in misery, and Jose thought the pain in his home was
normal. His father, an alcoholic, sometimes battered Jose's

mother severely. Over the years she suffered broken bones, bruises, and even a concussion from her husband's beatings. He was emotionally abusive as well, threatening his wife and telling her she was stupid or ugly. As she begged and pleaded not to be hit, Jose and his sister would run to their rooms to hide. The beatings occurred several times a year. Afterward Jose's father would apologize, bring the mother expensive gifts they couldn't afford, and promise to stop drinking. After a few months, however, the drinking would start and the beatings would follow.

Jose had the mistaken belief that if his mother would do what his father wanted, he would not start drinking again and there would be no more beatings. In Jose's culture, the woman was supposed to do as she was told and the man was supposed to be the boss. However, Jose did not realize that the beatings in his family were not culturally supported.

When Jose's parents' married, his mother was young, uneducated, and unemployable—or so she thought. She looked to her husband, who was quite a bit older, to tell her what to do. As she became more educated, more knowledgeable, and emotionally stronger she realized she no longer had to take her husband's emotional and physical abuse. Finally, she went with the children to a battered women's shelter. She already had a job, and the shelter helped her find inexpensive housing and legal counsel. She filed for separation and eventually a divorce.

Jose could not adjust to the changes in his family. He could not understand why his sister was not as upset about the divorce as he was. He could not understand that separating from an abusive father could be the best thing for the family. In his mind, the abuse was his mother's fault, it was her fault they left their home, and it was her fault that they were getting a divorce.

Since his father was no longer present, Jose felt he

needed to be the man of the house. Inappropriate as it was, so did his mother. She began to rely on him even though he was only eleven, going on twelve. She started to relate to him the way she had to her husband, begging him to do things as if she were a subordinate rather than his mother.

"I didn't know what to think. Sometimes she talked to me as if I were her child, and other times it seemed she talked to me as she would to Dad. Sometimes I thought I should hit her the way Dad did, but I couldn't, so I'd run away. I'd run to Dad's house. He would call her names and belittle her like he used to. I'd stay there for a few weeks, then Mom would beg me to come back and I'd go. The truth is, I didn't like to stay at Dad's. He had begun drinking more, and he'd start in on me the way he used to do to Mom. Also, he lived in a real rough neighborhood. There were a lot of gangs, and if I didn't want to get hurt I had to hang around with the gang. Sometimes it was okay, a way out of the house, but those guys would cause trouble. That's where I started smoking pot at twelve. They got me to skip school and hang out and smoke and drink. During one of my stays at Dad's, Mom got real worried and called social services. They tried to put me in foster care, but I didn't want to go. My uncle stepped in and said he would take me for a while, but he tricked me. He took me straight to a drug and alcohol treatment center.

"I stayed at the center for about two months, until Dad's insurance money ran out. It did me some good—I mean, I learned life could be okay without drugs—but I went back to drinking as soon as I got out. After six months I started smoking joints again too, but I never really got into it like before. Eventually, I quit pot altogether. I guess I was doing it to be like the other guys."

Jose perpetuated the conflict between his parents after they separated. He did not know that his mother had been receiving counseling before the separation; his mother was prepared to leave, but Jose was not. Struggling to make his needs known, Jose continued to encourage the conflict between his parents in an attempt to be in control.

"After rehab, I went back to my mom's, but I hated her rules. She wouldn't let me hang out at all. So I ran away. They put me in a shelter home for two months. Then I went back to Dad's. He used me to try to hurt Mom, so I felt bad and went back to Mom's. Two months later I'd get fed up with Mom's rules again and run away. I'd be back in the shelter and then back to Dad's. I did this for eighteen months. I was in the shelter at least nine times.

"Then things got worse. Mom started dating this guy I hated. He was real strict and backed up Mom's rules when I was there. I decided to get even, so I broke into his car and stole his radio. He filed charges against me—I couldn't believe it! That made me hate him more. The cops sent me to the detention center, where I stayed for a couple of days; then I went to court and was put on probation. That kind of shaped me up for a while. By then, Mom was living with this guy. When they decided to get married I started hanging out again, drinking, smoking, and skipping school. I don't know how, but I still got passing grades. I was so mad at them that I wanted to screw up everything, so I hung out a lot, but I still liked school because it seemed that people there liked me.

"Mom and my stepfather didn't like my attitude, so they kicked me out. I was fifteen. I went to Dad's again, but he had lost his job and was always complaining about money and that I ate too much. Eventually I went to live with friends and stayed with them as long as I could. I didn't know it at the time, but my mother was keeping an eye on me and giving them money for food. I guess she thought it was a safe place for me. But after a while I thought I had better leave, so I went out on the streets. It was summer, and there were others like me hanging around. I wasn't old enough for a regular job, so I started stealing stuff like radios and sports equipment so I could get a little weed, a little food, and a little drink. I was careful not to steal big items. After a few weeks I got tired of the life and stole a car, knowing I'd get caught. The court sent me to detention again, and this time they were rougher on me. I knew that would be the last time I would ever go there. Sometimes I seem like a tough guy, but I really do like the comforts of home. That kind of running wasn't for me anymore.

"I went back to Mom's again. My sister and I got into it one day, and I punched her. Not bad, but it was still a punch. It scared the heck out of me, and I knew I had to make some changes. I didn't know how to go about it, but I made up mind this was no way to live.

"I decided that I wanted to make it at home. School had just started, and I thought maybe I could make a new start. I was a sophomore and had always been athletic. I had been working out on weights all summer, and when I tried out for football I did great. I got a girlfriend who was really nice, and I got a part-time job at an auto parts store. Things were looking up. I had a little money and we could go out and have a good time. I stopped hanging out with the guys on the streets. Instead, I stayed after school and worked out on the weights, or went to work. After football season was over, a coach asked if I'd try out for wrestling. It turned out to be the sport for me.

"Mom lived in a nicer area than Dad. I don't mean rich or anything, but people seemed to care a little more about their place. There was no trash on the street, and stuff like that. It seems to me that some people in the poor areas of town do all right, but others seem depressed, angry, or jealous when they don't have much. It seemed like I got to feeling that way too when I was with Dad. I also feel a lot better about myself when I work out. If I'm really mad and I spend an hour on the weight machines, I don't feel much like fighting anymore.

"My coaches in particular cared about what I did. The more effort I put out, the more they seemed to care. They told me I had talent, and that made me feel really good about myself.

"When I turned seventeen, things got a little rough at home again, and I wanted to be on my own. I wanted more freedom than Mom would give me, but I didn't want to get back into old habits. Over the last year or so we had been involved in a family therapy program, sort of on and off. We discussed this in therapy and came up with a plan. There was an opening in an independent living program, and since I had been working and staying in school, I was a good candidate. The county would help financially for me to live in an apartment for six months. I had to stay in school and work part time, and by the time the six months was over I would have graduated from high school. It sounded like something I could handle, so my parents agreed, although somewhat reluctantly. It was better than having me just take off on my own."

Jose was successful in the program and has done a good job of preparing to be on his own. In school his grades were so-so, but good enough to graduate. His sports achievements helped him feel self-confident and gave him a way to handle stress; and his part-time job experience was positive, giving him good work references. Jose feels good about his accomplishments and looks forward to graduating.

His relationships still need some work. Although his family relationships are better, there is still a lot of conflict.

He often finds himself in the middle between his mom and dad, and there are problems with his stepfather because of that. If Jose wants to alter patterns of conflict already established by his family, he will have to work hard at it. However, it may take a major crisis in his life to motivate him to change. Like most people, it is easier for Jose to avoid the pain of his past than to face up to and correct his problems. At some time in his life, probably in a relationship with a girlfriend, the patterns of Jose's family life will surface and he will be forced to handle it or continue his own family in the same pattern he grew up with.

PROBLEM AREAS

Growing Up in a Home with Violence

Jose grew up learning that violence gets you what you want. In his home, might equaled right. Although he himself was not abused, Jose learned that it was okay to hit those you love. Society does not condone violence within the family. Although it is acceptable in certain instances such as during war, in self-defense, and as part of sports, rules must be followed for such accepted violence. The violence Jose grew up with had no rules and was not acceptable.

As a teenager, Jose was often at odds with people in authority. Parents, teachers, police, and others in charge didn't know who Jose really was because early in life he had learned to act any part to get what he wanted. In the street he needed to be tough and fierce with the gang, and he played the part convincingly no matter how scared he was. At other times he could be charming, such as when he needed a favor from a teacher. "Sometimes even I didn't know the real Jose. I'd sometimes switch from being tough to charming in a matter of minutes if it meant my survival." After intensive therapy, Jose learned how to deal effectively with others so that he could safely present the "real" Jose and still get what he wanted a good portion of the time.

Jose described his feelings after his dad left. "I couldn't get close to anyone. I never could really trust them. When I was a little older, I felt I could trust my coaches a little, but I was always half expecting they would turn on me.

"My first girlfriend, Rosa, told me I always kept a distance. She'd do everything for me, and I did little back. I never did feel close the way you should with a girlfriend. I still don't know if I could. I might get swallowed up or maybe so hurt I couldn't stand it."

Teens who have been emotionally abandoned in childhood frequently feel this way. However, it is extremely difficult for human beings to survive and succeed without relying on others for support and caring. Jose will have to learn to let others into his life if he wishes to do well and feel good about himself.

Drug and Alcohol Abuse

Jose has had trouble coping with drug and alcohol abuse. Fortunately, he has stayed away from hard drugs such as crack and heroin. "I think I was a prime candidate for using cocaine, but I simply didn't have the money. Also, I didn't want any more jail time, and I knew my family would give up on me if I got into the hard stuff."

Jose will likely continue his substance abuse unless he learns to understand his need for drugs and alcohol and takes clear action to eliminate his use. He says that he smokes marijuana mainly when the other guys are using it. "It's a social thing. I figure I can stop any time. To prove it, I don't use it when I'm on a team." That may be so for marijuana, but more likely it will be harder than he thinks.

Alcohol abuse is a concern that will affect Jose his entire life. His father is an alcoholic. Many studies on generational abuse of alcohol confirm that there is a strong connection between parent and child. The risk of alcohol abuse increases tenfold for the child of an alcoholic parent. That child then carries the problem into the family he or she establishes, and the trend is continued.

Using Behavior to Control Others

Jose learned early in life that he could manipulate and control others through negative behavior. For instance, if he ran away he could get many family members involved in the search. One time he just hid up in a tree near his house and watched everyone search frantically for him. Jose felt he had to act out to get his emotional needs met, and his negative behaviors usually increased when his parents were in their fighting phases. He wanted attention, but he also thought that if he created a distraction he could get his parents to stop fighting. Eventually his family paid less and less attention to his acting out, and the more he tried to control others, the less influence he had. It wasn't that Jose was a bad kid; in fact people meeting him for the first time were often impressed by his pleasantness. Rather, he got involved in bad activities to survive emotionally in his family.

Living in a chaotic and inconsistent family, Jose did not develop a sense of belonging and safety. Rather than acquiring a tradition of values supporting the individual in the family, Jose acquired values that demean and intimidate. His negative behavior was a symptom of his feeling of powerlessness to affect his world. Jose and many foster teens are forced into adulthood early without experiencing the transition from childhood that adolescence usually provides. They are often asked to make adult decisions about their lives without adequate experience or self-control.

Jose will have to be careful about his stored-up anger. When he perceives that people have failed him, he will likely react with anger that appears excessive to the cause. He will have to be very careful not to repeat his father's pattern of violence.

THINGS THAT HELPED

Alternative High School

Jose fortunately lived in a school district with an alternative high school program. Alternative high schools, part of the special education program, are designed to meet the needs of students who are at high risk of not completing high school. Many students, some of whom are very bright yet unmotivated in a traditional school program, need the smaller teacher-student ratio of the alternative school that provides more interactive and creative outlets. Some need remedial work in such areas as math or language. Education is geared to the student who wants to learn and graduate.

Physical Conditioning

In searching for activities to replace his high school athletics, Jose joined a gym and took part in a physical conditioning and weight lifting program. He received a great deal of encouragement from the staff, entered several tournaments, and did quite well. Weight lifting enabled Jose to feel good about himself, strengthen himself, and thus increase his self-esteem.

Many teens like Jose gravitate toward peers who participate in such antisocial activities as stealing and drug and alcohol abuse. Physical programs provide a healthy alternative. Anyone who has received treatment for drug or alcohol use needs to surround himself with people who encourage him to make good choices.

Genograms and Lifelines

In a seminar Jose attended he learned of the generational alcohol abuse in his family by making a genogram. Similar to a family tree, a genogram details a family's health data, major illnesses, divorces, and other significant family occurrences.

Jose's genogram, portraying problems areas such as anniversary dates affecting all family members, demonstrated the need for intervention in his case.

Another way to track and examine pertinent family information is to draw a Lifeline, which tracks significant events in a person's life. Lifelines include birthdays, hospitalizations, sibling births, major moves, and other significant events. Anniversaries of significant or traumatic events often bring depression; likewise, if something good happened on a particular day, one might feel good or confident on that anniversary. Lifelines can help teens know these dates and understand the feelings they may cause.

JOSE'S LIFELINE

BIRTHDAY 9-23-73

AGE 1	10-73	I was hospitalized for 3 wks for pneumonia
	12-73	Mom hospitalized for appendicitis stayed with grandmom for 3 wks
AGE 2	12-74	Mom hospitalized for 3 wks don't know why—stayed with grandmom
AGE 3	6-75	Dad in hospital—car accident alcohol related
AGE 4	7-2-77	Sister, Teresa, born Mom in hospital 7 days
	7-25-77	Mom hospitalized 3 days infection stayed with grandmom 3 wks
AGE 5	10-77	Hospitalized for tonsillectomy
	12-77	Dad broke Mom's arm
	6-78	Camping that summer
AGE 6	6-79	Camp
	9-79	Started school—awful
AGE 7	6-80	Dad left for 2 wks. Mom made him leave—Hit Mom with bottle
AGE 8	5-1-81	Dad beat Mom up—Dad left
	6-81	Dad hospitalized—hepatitis
	7-81	Camp
AGE 9	6-82	Dad & Mom's divorce final
AGE 10	10-83	Tom moved in with Mom
	12-83	I ran away
AGE 11	6-12-84	Tom & Mom marry
	6-84	I moved in with Dad
	7-84	Moved back with Mom

BIRTHDAY 9-23-73 (con't)

AGE 12	3-12-85	Sister, Sonja, born
	6-85	Uncle took me to detox
	10-85	Arrested

AGE 13	1-86	Moved back with Dad
	2-86	Punched Tom, kicked out
	3-86	Met girlfriend Lynn
	6-86	Picked up for shoplifting

AGE 14	7-86	Placed in shelter
	9-86	Group home placement
	12-86	Went to Mom's
	1-87	Went to Dad's
	2-87	Went to Grandmom's

AGE 15	3-87	Went to Mom's
	4-87	Went to Dad's
	5-87	Went to Shelter
	6-87	Went to Mom's
	7-87	Went to Uncle

AGE 16	8-87	Ran away
	1-88	Went to Shelter
	2-88	Went to Dad
	3-88	Went to Mom's
	10-88	Went to Dad

AGE 17	1-89	Got job
	2-89	Got apartment
	5-89	Got Sport award

CHAPTER 7

Mutual Care

L aTara, a black seventeen-year-old, was eleven when she first entered foster care. "I can only remember back to when I was nine years old. I don't know why, but I can't remember before that. I remember some beatings my mom gave me then, but I guess they probably started before that."

It is not uncommon for foster teens to have memory blanks. A person should be able to remember at least to age five, and most can remember special events as early as age three. LaTara no doubt experienced events that were so scary or hurtful that she repressed them.

"I never told anyone but my sister about the beatings. If I had bruises or scratches, I hid them so the teachers at school wouldn't notice. I was usually a quiet kid and never got into trouble, so no one ever even noticed.

"Then it got too bad at home. I remember the day very well. On December 16, when I was eleven, we had a Christmas program at school and I had a very good part. My sister and I were in the bathroom getting ready for the program. I knew Mom was doing drugs, and we usually stayed out of her way when she did them, but that day the smell of marijuana was real strong. We didn't want Mom to come to the program because she always acted weird when she took drugs, but we didn't want to hurt her feelings either. When my sister said something about Mom not coming, Mom came into the bathroom swinging a broom. She broke my sister's nose. Sis was bleeding real bad, and that freaked Mom out. She started screaming like a banshee and hitting me with the heel of her shoe. She busted my head, which later needed three stitches. We still wanted to go to the play, so somehow we cleaned ourselves up, but Mom didn't want us to go so she started swinging a belt at us. We ran upstairs and climbed out the third-floor window. There was an abandoned grocery cart outside, so I got in it and my sister pushed me all the way to school. When we got there one of the teachers took us to the emergency room. There they called a social worker, who took us to foster care.

"I wish it hadn't happened then. It seems like every year before Christmas I remember that day. I get real depressed and usually pick a fight with someone. I never can have a happy holiday with that memory hanging over my head.

"At first the social worker sent us to a shelter home. This was to be temporary, and they were able to find a group home for my sister real quick. But I was too young for a group home, and they had a hard time finding a place for a black girl in our community. So I stayed in the shelter for three months. I took a bus to my old school every day until I moved to a long-term foster home. It used to take me nearly an hour to get to school and to get back. It was a good thing I liked school."

LaTara has bad memories of her first foster home. "At first my foster parents seemed nice, but the mom was too sensitive. She was always getting her feelings hurt. She always wanted me to talk about my problems, but I didn't want to and neither did the other foster kids. When we wouldn't talk, she'd do nasty things to us, like she might take her own kids to a show and make us stay home."

LaTara, a very quiet girl, found it difficult to talk to anyone. She had spent most of her childhood not telling anyone what was going on in her life for fear of reprisals. Talking to this stranger, her foster mother, was extremely scary for a girl who had learned to trust no one.

"I finally had it with my foster mom and ran away, but I came back a week later. I didn't think she would take me back, but she did. Looking back now, I wish I hadn't gone back; maybe my life would have been different.

"I decided to try to talk to her, but whenever I was ready she was busy. Maybe I picked busy times like when she was making dinner because I really didn't really want to talk. Sometimes she scolded me for things I told her. She was very religious, and I hated that. When I would tell her something a little off-color that had happened at school, she would become very angry.

"Another big problem was that she wanted me to call her 'Mom,' but I didn't want to. When I called her by her first name, she got mad. I made up a silly name for her, and she still got mad. I tried to tell her that I had a mother who let me down and I didn't want to call anyone Mom, but she didn't buy it. We fought over that a lot."

Calling the foster mother "Mom" became a very big problem for LaTara. If the title is a problem, the foster teen should talk to the social worker and make arrangements that satisfy both the teen and the parents. There are so many more important concerns to worry about. For LaTara, this issue was a smokescreen for other more important worries, many which never got discussed. A teen's first placement, if the setting is supportive, is the perfect opportunity for helping professionals to determine the painful experiences that the child has endured. If the abuses are discovered early, future abuse patterns and problems can be prevented.

Since LaTara was unable to talk about the things that truly worried her, she hung on to her history of abuse and it disrupted her teen years. Years later it was revealed that her "uncle"—an ex-boyfriend of her mother's—had sexually molested LaTara on many occasions over the period of a year. He threatened that if she told anyone she would be taken away to live in a group home and would never see her family again. LaTara believed him. "What I should have done the first time he tried to touch me was run and get help, but I didn't know. I was scared. He was someone I knew and had trusted, so I thought he must be right. After a while he gave me nice things. He brought me beautiful dolls and clothes, things my mother couldn't afford. I don't think my mother knew about it, but if she did I don't know if she would have been able to stop him. I found out later that it happened to her too when she was young, and she was unable to stop it."

LaTara only recently shared this secret. The years she held it in kept her from getting the help she needed; because of the repression of the early painful memories, LaTara made many decisions that disrupted her life forever.

LaTara observed, "Had I gotten the help I needed, my life would have been so different. Perhaps it could have been like other teenagers'."

LaTara knows of what she speaks. Her "uncle" eventually moved away, but even after he left, the hurt, the shame, and the guilt remained. LaTara also had learned that sexual activity got her the attention she desired, and she continued to be sexually active even before she reached puberty.

When she went into foster care, her feelings of loneliness and emptiness increased, and she thought sexual activity would make her feel cared about. She recalls sneaking out of the foster home at night. "I started hanging out with older kids. They would use me and then lose me. I got hurt over and over again, but I kept thinking that each guy might be different. After getting caught sneaking out, I'd be grounded. When I ditched classes I got suspended. I was sort of driven, and I wasn't able to get what I really wanted—to be loved and have someone care about me.

"Then I became pregnant, and my boyfriend denied he was the father, saying I did it with everyone. Actually, I wasn't sure who the father was; no one wanted the responsibility and no one wanted me."

LaTara became very confused. "I didn't think I should have an abortion. I believed it was the wrong thing to do, but I knew I couldn't raise a child. My family had long since abandoned me. I only half trusted my foster mom, but she was all I had. She told me that black people don't give up their babies and said she'd help me raise the baby. So that's what I did. The pregnancy was difficult, and I was considered high risk for problems since I was so young. The doctors had to check me every other week, and I guess I did like all the attention. Everyone I knew was concerned and worried about me. I had more phone calls and visitors than I ever had before. The pregnancy made me feel important, but that feeling was only temporary.

"The delivery was very difficult. My body was not mature enough to deliver a baby, and I had to have a C-section. The baby, four weeks early, had problems too. She had trouble breathing because of her undeveloped lungs. My recovery was hard, and I cried and cried. I didn't want to see the baby or take her home, but everyone said they would help."

They did help for a while. Recovery was slow for LaTara, and both she and the baby needed a lot of care. She got a great deal of attention for the next few months. As LaTara grew well, however, the attention diminished and she was required to take more responsibility in caring for the baby. LaTara resisted. "I needed to go out and be with my friends, not be tied down to a baby. The school had a young mothers program in which a mother could bring her baby to school, go to classes, and take care of the baby too, but I didn't want to do that. I just wanted to hang out with my friends and let my foster mother take care of the baby. I was also supposed to go to a group for young mothers at social services. I went once and they did a lot of fun things, but when it really got down to it I didn't want to be a mother at all. I mean I loved the baby and all, but I needed too much myself.

"One day the foster mom complained about my care of the baby and how I seemed to be neglecting her. When she said she wanted to adopt the baby, I panicked. I didn't want the baby, but I sure as heck didn't want her to be the baby's mother. I really hated her. So I took the baby and ran away. I had no idea how I was going to survive or even where I'd go. I went to the mall and hung around until I saw a friend, who took me home. The baby cried all the time, and I didn't know how to make her stop. I was scared. My friend's mother called my social worker, and she arranged for me to stay there until she could find another place. I refused to go back to my old foster home."

Social services eventually placed LaTara in a special mutual care foster home, allowing her and her infant to live with a trained foster family.

LaTara said, "For the first time I really enjoyed a foster home. Before, I never felt like I fitted in. My previous foster mother always tried to change me, but my new parents accepted me for who I was, and because of that I wanted to please them. They took good care of both me and my baby, and they helped me to be more patient with the baby. Mostly, they listened to me and I felt they truly heard me. I wasn't ready to be a parent, no matter what anyone said or how guilty my old foster mom made me feel. I did not want to be a mother, and the guilt was always there. My old foster mom kept saying to me in my mind, 'Black people don't give up their babies.'

"With the help and support of the new foster parents and my social worker, I realized that I could not give the baby what she needed, and I knew I didn't want her to have a mother like I had. She needed so much more. Finally I made the decision I had actually made at her birth to place her for adoption. She was seven months old, and although I don't think it did any of us any good to wait so long, I was really pleased to have been able to get to know her. I gave her to parents who were older and who could give her the good life I knew I couldn't.

"When I met the adoptive family, they decided to keep the name I had given the baby, which made me happy. At least, she would have something I gave her. I made a little book for her with pictures and names of me and my family, so when she got bigger she would know what I looked like. I wrote about our family history and also our medical problems. I told her that I loved her and wanted her to have a good life. It really helped me to say good-bye, knowing she would learn that I was not an awful person."

There are many ways a child may be given up for adoption. In open adoptions, birth parents and parents keep in touch; in closed adoptions the child has very little knowledge of the natural parents other than medical and physical information. LaTara chose something in the middle. She met the adoptive parents, and her child will have some information about her and where to find her if she wants to; but she also chose to have no contact with her after the adoption. LaTara felt satisfied that her decision was best for her and her child.

Despite this, LaTara was extremely sad. "I cried for weeks. I'm not sure why, because it was what I wanted. In a way, I felt like she had died or at least had left my world. I was able to continue at the foster home even though I no longer had my child with me, and I was really glad. With that foster family I became a better student and I stopped ditching. I started to enjoy being a teenager. I stayed with that family until I was sixteen; then it seemed like it was time for me to go. I'm not sure why, because I could have stayed there until I was eighteen. I was placed in an independent living program where I was helped with the rent while I attended school. After eight months I had to support myself; then things got harder. Now I don't have a job, and I'm living with my boyfriend. He's really nice to me, and I just found out I'm pregnant. I know I'm still young, but this time I feel I'm ready to be a mother. My boyfriend is excited and plans to be there for me. He's older and has a pretty good job."

As soon as LaTara left the foster home, the empty feelings returned. She sought to fill the void once again. Lynn Mullen, a social worker in a mutual care program in Colorado, finds that young teens in foster care typically repeat pregnancies. "I believe these young women come from emotionally deprived families to begin with. When they are pregnant they receive attention they never received before, and they enjoy it. Subconsciously they repeat pregnancy in hope of again receiving attention, not thinking through the consequences."

Will LaTara at seventeen be any more ready to care for a baby? She appears to be more committed this time, and that may make a difference. She has a little more support in that her boyfriend is taking some responsibility. Yet LaTara has not yet learned how to take care of herself and how to get her needs met in a healthy and appropriate manner. She lost her childhood and is trying to hang onto it in an ineffective manner. LaTara may be able to take care of this baby, and she may do well. Or she may have trouble and have to give the child up at a later date. Or she may hurt the baby later on in life as LaTara's mother hurt her, repeating the cycle. In any event, the path LaTara has chosen is a difficult one.

PROBLEM AREAS

LaTara not only had to cope with many of the problems described previously such as relationships, trust, and a chaotic childhood, but she also had problems unique to her.

Early Pregnancy

U.S. government population studies show that nearly one in four fifteen-year-olds are sexually active. In foster care it has been observed that nearly three out of four fifteen-year-olds are or have been sexually active, and nearly all foster teens have been exposed to inappropriate sexual activity such as assault or molestation, or pornographic exploitation.

LaTara was especially vulnerable to the problems of teenage pregnancy because of her youth. Infants of very young mothers have increased risk of infant death, premature delivery—as in LaTara's case—and congenital birth defects. Childbirth has a profound effect on any mother, but with early pregnancy it can be devastating.

Frequently the mother is forced to drop out of school. If she decides to keep her child, she is often too young to work and is forced to live a minimal existence on welfare. For a woman having a first child as a young teen, the chance of infant death in subsequent pregnancies also increases. Young bodies, not sufficiently developed to carry the weight of a fetus, can develop lifelong physical problems.

Pregnancy for most teens is a time of disbelief, denial, fear, anger, depression, and dread. Underlying emotional problems, usually the cause of the unprotected sexual activity, usually come to the forefront. Regardless of whether the teen chooses to keep the baby, place the baby in an adoptive home, or have an abortion, the pregnancy will change her life forever. She will often feel guilty and depressed with the nagging question, "Did I make the right choice?"

Not Fitting In

LaTara once said of her first foster families, "Even though they tried very hard to make me a part of the family, I never felt I really belonged."

LaTara's feeling of not belonging, common for foster teens, is often accompanied by feelings of inadequacy. Such teens believe they are defective because they are not with their family. "How could Mom let this happen to me? I must be an awful person if I can't be with her."

Not wanting to get close to anyone, some teens work to keep the foster family at an emotional distance. LaTara recalls, "I always felt like a visitor in my foster homes. I didn't want to get close to anyone. I didn't think anyone really wanted me around since my mother didn't."

Despite what some foster parents say, foster teens know

that they are not really a family member and may be forced to move on the whim of an adult. Although they know they are not biological children, they still want to be treated fairly.

"At my last foster home," LaTara recalls, "I felt the best. My foster family were great. They included me in their activities, accepted me for who I was, and treated me fairly. Maybe because they were white and I was black, they never tried to force me into feeling like I was their blood. We knew I was different and accepted it."

Loss

Like the other foster teens, LaTara was faced with feelings of abandonment by her mother. She knew her mother used drugs and was aware of what drugs did to people's judgment; still she felt betrayed. Her mother rarely visited her in foster care and followed none of the treatment plans outlined in court. Now LaTara lives with her boyfriend just a few blocks from her mother's house and secretly hopes that someday her mother will drop by and make up for all those years. LaTara believes her life would have been different had her mother taken care of her properly.

LaTara also felt abandoned when she put her own child up for adoption. Wishing they could somehow keep their child, most teen mothers feel tremendous emotional pain as they place their child in an adoptive home. Despite the pain, LaTara acted out of love, hoping the child would have a better home than she could provide.

Facing abandonment by her own mother and her baby, LaTara repeated her mistake and became pregnant a second time. Unfortunately, statistics indicate that it will be very hard for LaTara to raise this second child. Her boyfriend probably won't be around by the time the baby is born, and LaTara is still not mature enough to raise a child on her own. Since she has chosen to be on her own, mutual care foster homes are no longer available to her. She won't be able to finish high school, and she will probably have to go on welfare.

LaTara appears more committed to this child, and community resources will be available to her. But even if she raises the child past infancy, LaTara will no doubt be reminded of her painful experiences and repeat the mistakes of her own mother.

THINGS THAT HELPED

Mutual Care Program

For LaTara, the special foster care program was exactly what she needed. The program provides a teen mother with medical assistance, psychological counseling, assistance in finding appropriate school or job programs, day care, and parenting skill classes. Foster parents in this program receive special training to understand the needs of the child.

Some programs provide groups for teen mothers for socializing and learning parenting skills. Lynne Mullen manages such a program. "Over the years I have supervised many groups for teen mothers. I began to realize that they had so many emotional needs of their own that focusing on the needs of their infant was very hard. Now our groups focus on the mothers as well, letting them have some fun and addressing their individual needs and worries. As they learn better social skills, they also learn more effective means of meeting their emotional needs. Growing stronger and more confident, the girls become better parents through this approach."

Because LaTara benefited so much from this program, she continued in it even after she placed her baby for adoption. The group helped her deal with her feelings about the adoption and supported her through her grief. LaTara recalls, "I learned so much from the others in the group. I don't know how I could have made it without them. I know I'll be able to use what I learned with my next child."

Summary

Even at its best, foster care is difficult and demanding for the most resourceful teen. At first most of them feel lost, desperately wishing they could be somewhere else. Although foster care may provide relief from an abusive situation, even those teens feel hurt, disappointment, and a sense of abandonment by their birth family. Fortunately many foster teens go on to develop strong positive relationships with their caretakers, allowing the teens to grow into adulthood with a sense of accomplishment and self-confidence.

For success in foster care, teens need courage, commitment to self, and clear thinking. Developing trust—which is most difficult as one is faced with many strangers with different value systems—allows the teen to take advantage of what foster care can provide. A strong belief in self also permits the teen to carry on despite many losses and disappointments.

Foster teens have tried in many ways to help themselves. Some have worked; others have not. The things that have worked best are talking to professionals—counselors, teachers, or other responsible adults; writing about their feelings; participating in community support groups such as AA, school and church activities, and sports or exercise programs; and participating in foster family activities or programs designed to improve relationships with birth families.

Successful foster teens develop positive relationships with other teens who do well in school and at home. They learn to make good choices in friends and accept themselves as good people who have something to contribute to their family, their friends, and their community. The Appendix lists many resources that are available to foster teens as they strive to accomplish their goals.

Glossary

adoption   Legal parental relationship between nonbiologically related adult or adults and a child.

adoptee   Adopted child.

biofather or birth father   Biological father.

biomother or birth mother   Biological mother.

caseworker/social worker: Agency worker assigned to maintain case records, talk with family members and other involved parties, and report to the court system when required by law.

child neglect   Failure of parent or legal guardian to provide for a child's basic physical, educational, or emotional needs by not providing or by delaying appropriate health care; allowing chronic truancy; failing to enroll child in school; allowing chronic spouse abuse in front of child; knowingly allowing child to use drugs or alcohol; refusing to provide psychological care if needed.

emotional abuse   Acts or omissions that have caused or could cause serious behavioral, cognitive, emotional, or mental dysfunctions.

foster home, therapeutic foster home   Parent, set of parents, or family who provides parental care to an unrelated child; therapeutic foster homes meet the exceptional psychological needs of a disadvantaged child on a 24-hour basis.

group home   Facility supervised by individuals, couples, or staff members who oversee and provide parental care to unrelated children.

mutual care foster home   Foster home that provides parental care for an unwed teen mother and infant child.

physical abuse   Infliction of physical injury on a child by parent, guardian, or caretaker.

placement   Act of placing a child in a foster home or adoptive home.

psychiatric hospitalization   Placement of a person in a hospital because of concern about emotional stability.

relinquishment of parental rights   Legal term used when one or both legal parents give up rights to their child to the court system.

sexual abuse   Wide range of behaviors by an adult to a child, including fondling of genitals, intercourse, rape, sodomy, exhibitionism, and commercial exploitation such as prostitution or pornography.

shelter care, shelter home, receiving home   Short-term housing facility for teens.

termination of parental rights   Legal transfer of parental rights to the court system; this transfer is involuntary.

Appendix

HELPING RESOURCES

Runaway Hotlines

Department of Health and Human Services
Division of Runaway Youth Program
Washington, DC
(202) 755-7800

Child Help—USA
(800) 422-4453
(800) 4-A-Child

Child Find
P.O. Box 277
New Paltz, NY
(800) 648-3463

Help, Inc.
638 South Street
Philadelphia, PA 19147
(215) 542-7766
24-hour hotline

Missing Children—Help Center
410 Ware Boulevard
Tampa, FL 33619
(813) 623-5437

National Center for Missing and Exploited Children
1835 K Street NW
Washington, DC 20006
(202) 634-9821
(800) 843-5678
(800) 843-5679

National Runaway Hotline
(800) 621-4000
In Illinois (800) 972-6004

Operation: Peace of Mind
(800) 231-6946
In Texas: (800) 392-3352
In Alaska and Hawaii: (800) 231-6762
24-hour hotline to promote communication between parents and
  teens who do not want to divulge their location

National Runaway Switchboard
(800) 621-4000
Offers crisis help and referral services

Temporary Shelters

Alternative House
McClean, VA
(703) 356-2045

Children of the Night
1800 North Highland Avenue
Hollywood, CA 90028
(213) 461-3160
Protection and shelter for children and teens 8–17 involved in
  prostitution and/or pornography.

Help, Inc.
638 South Street
Philadelphia, PA 19147
(215) 546-7766
Runaway house, medical clinic, counseling center.

Suicide Hotlines

National Adolescent Suicide Hotline
(800) 621-4000

National Institute of Mental Health
(301) 443-4515

Listed by State
Hope Line
3807 McCain Park Drive
North Little Rock, AR 72116
(501) 758-6922

Suicide Prevention and Crisis Center for San Mateo County
1811 Trousdale Drive
Burlingame, CA 94010
(415) 877-5604

Monterey County Suicide Prevention Center
P.O. Box 3241
Carmel, CA 93921
(408) 375-6966

Suicide Prevention Service of Sacramento County
P.O. Box 449
Sacramento, CA 95802
(916) 441-1138

Pueblo Suicide Prevention Center
229 Colorado Avenue
Pueblo, CO 81004
(303) 545-2477

Suicide and Crisis Control
2459 South Ash
Denver, CO 80222
(303) 746-8485
(303) 757-0988

InfoLine of SW Connecticut
7 Academy Street
Norwalk, CT 06850
(203) 853-9109

The Wheeler Clinic—Emergency Services
91 Northwest Drive
Plainville, CT 06062
(203) 747-6801

Psychiatric Emergency Services
2001 North DuPont Parkway
New Castle, DE 19720
(302) 656-4428

Suicide Prevention Service
801 North Capillary Street NE
Washington, DC 20002
(202) 629-5222

Personal Crisis Services
30 East Eighth Street
Miami, FL 33131
(305) 379-2611

We Care, Inc.
610 Mariposa
Orlando, FL 32801
(305) 241-3329

Helpline
1512 Bull Street
Savannah, GA 31401
(912) 232-3383

Suicide and Crisis Center
200 North Vineyard Boulevard
Honolulu, HI 96817
(808) 521-4555

Crisis Intervention Services
4200 North Oak Park Avenue
Chicago, IL 60634
(312) 794-3609

Call for Help
320 East Armstrong Avenue
Peoria, IL 61603
(309) 691-7373
(309) 691-7374

Suicide Prevention Center
250 North 17th Street
Kansas City, KS 66102
(913) 371-7171

Can Help
Topeka, KS 66604
(913) 235-3434
(913) 235-3435

Crisis Line
1528 Jackson Avenue
New Orleans, LA 70130
(504) 523-4446

Adolescent Center
Boston City Hospital
818 Harrison Avenue
Boston, MA
(617) 426-6068

Crisis Intervention Center
Minneapolis, MN 55415
(612) 330-7777
(612) 330-7780

Listening Post
Meridian, MS 39301
(601) 693-1001

Children's Hospital
Detroit, MI
(313) 494-5762

Western Missouri Suicide Center
600 East 22nd Street
Kansas City, MO 64108
(816) 471-3000

Great Falls Crisis Center
Great Falls, MT 59401

Omaha Personal Crisis Center
Omaha, NE 68101
(402) 342-6290

Suicide Prevention and Crisis Call Center
Reno, NV 89581
(702) 323-6111

Crisis Referral and Information
232 East Front Street
Plainfield, NJ 07060
(201) 561-4800

Adolescent Clinic
Martland Hospital
100 Bergen Street
Newark, NJ
(201) 456-5779

Adolescent Medical Program
Brookdale Hospital
Brooklyn, NY 11212
(718) 240-6452

Montefiore Hospital
111 East 210th Street
Bronx, NY 10467

Roosevelt Hospital
428 West 59th Street
New York, NY 10019
(212) 545-7475

The Door
618 Avenue of Americas
New York, NY 10011
(212) 691-6161

W.F. Ryan Teen Center
160 West 100th Street
New York, NY 10021
(212) 865-7661

Threshold
115 Clinton Avenue South
Rochester, NY 14604
(716) 454-7560

Fargo Clinic
737 Broadway
Fargo, ND 58102
(701) 237-2431

Findley Market Clinic
19 North Elder Street
Cincinnati, OH
(513) 621-4400

Cleveland Clinic Foundations
9500 Euclid Street
Cleveland, OH
(214) 444-5616

Children's Memorial Hospital
940 NE 13th Street
Oklahoma City, OK 73190
(405) 271-6208

Children's Hospital
34th & Civic Center Boulevard
Philadelphia, PA 19104
(215) 387-6311

Greenville General Hospital
Greenville, SC 29605
(803) 242-8625

Suicide and Crisis Intervention Service
Memphis, TN 38104
(901) 726-5534

Crisis Intervention Services
Corpus Christi, TX 78404
(512) 883-0271

Suicide Prevention of Dallas
Dallas, TX 75219
(214) 521-9111

Crisis Intervention of Houston
Houston, TX 72210
(713) 527-9864

Granite Community Mental Health Center
Salt Lake City, UT
(801) 484-8761

Suicide Crisis Center
Portsmouth, VA 23705
(804) 399-6395

Crisis Clinic
1530 Eastlake East
Seattle, WA 98102
(206) 329-1882

Suicide Prevention Services
Charleston, WV
(304) 346-3337

Emergency Services
31 South Henry Street
Madison, WI 53703
(608) 251-2341

Helpline
Cheyenne, WY 82001
(307) 634-4469

Services are also available at your local hospital.

Drug and Alcohol Assistance

National Clearinghouse on Drug and Alcohol Abuse
For information:
(301) 468-2600
(301) 443-2403
For treatment referral:
(800) 662-HELP
For referral of adolescent programs:
(301) 468-2600

Young People in AA
For referral information:
(212) 686-1100

Cocaine Anonymous
Call your local chapter or your AA chapter.

Coaches Program For Drug and Alcohol Prevention
(202) 633-1437

DO IT NOW Foundation
Peer-to-peer counseling and information concerning drugs.
(602) 257-0797

National Cocaine Hotline
(800) COCAINE

NAR-ANON
Helps families deal with drug abuse problems.
For information and referral information:
(213) 547-5800

AL-ANON and Teen ANON
For information and referral information:
(212) 302-7240
(212) 481-6565

Palmer Drug Abuse Programs
Rehabilitation programs throughout the country.
(213) 989-0902

Teen Pregnancy

Adolescent Pregnancy Programs
Public Health Service
Department of Health and Human Services
1330 Independence Avenue SW
Washington, DC
(202) 245-7473

Information on Sex and Teens

FIRST
Box 57
Sanford, NC 27330
(919) 774-9515

Teens helping teens understand the consequences of sex and
pregnancy.

Rape Information Clearinghouse
(301) 443-0353

National Abortion Federation Hotline
(800) 223-0618

National Association Concerned with School-Aged Parents
7315 Wisconsin Avenue
Washington, DC 20014

Counseling and Therapy Referrals

American Association for Marriage and Family Therapy
924 West 9th Street
Upland, CA 91786
(714) 981-0888

National Clearinghouse for Mental Health Information
(301) 443-4513
(301) 443-4514

Medical Concerns

National Associations of Anorexia Nervosa and Bulimia
(312) 831-3438

American Anorexic and Bulimic Association
(201) 836-1800

BASH
Self-help for bulimics
(800) 227-4785

National Health Information Clearinghouse
(800) 336-4797

TOTLINE
Counseling for young mothers.
(201) 442-1362

Venereal Disease Hotline
(800) 227-8922
In California:
(800) 982-5833

Legal

Children's Legal Rights Information
(202) 332-6575

Adoption

Adopted Teen Pen-Pal Club
P.O. Box LL
Wellfleet, MA 02667

Adoptee's Liberty Movement Association
P.O. Box 154, Washington Bridge Station
New York, NY
(212) 581-1568

Reunite Inc.
P.O. Box 694
Reynoldsburg, OH 43068
(614) 861-2584

Open Door Society—Adoption Warmline
(213) 402-3664

Further Reading

Adams, Caren; Fay, Jennifer; Loreen-Marten, Jan; and Hyde Margaret. *No Is Not Enough.* San Luis Obispo, CA: Impact Publishers, 1984.

Ashabranner, Brent and Melissa. *Into a Strange Land.* New York: Putnam Publishing Group, 1987.

Calvert, Patricia. *When Morning Comes* (fiction). New York: Macmillan, 1989.

Cohen, Shari. *Coping with Adoption.* New York: Rosen Publishing Group, 1988.

Cooney, Judith. *Coping with Sexual Abuse*, rev. ed. New York: Rosen Publishing Group, 1991.

King, Buzz. *Silicon Songs* (fiction). New York: Doubleday, 1990.

Mackey, Gene, and Swan, Helen. *Dear Elizabeth.* Kansas City, KS: Children's Institute, 1983.

McKay, Matthew. *When Anger Hurts.* Oakland, CA: New Harbinger Publications, 1989.

Olney, Ross Robert. *Up Against the Law.* New York: E. P. Dutton, 1985.

Rosenfeld, Linda. *Left Alive.* Springfield, IL: C. C. Thomas, 1984.

Ryerson, Eric. *When Your Parent Drinks Too Much.* New York: Warner Books, 1987.

Samuels, Gertrude. *Yours, Brett* (fiction). New York: Lodestar Books, 1988.

Terkel, Susan Neiburg. *Feeling Safe, Feeling Strong.* Minneapolis: Lerner Publications, 1984.

Wachter, Orales. *No More Secrets for Me* (Spanish). Barcelona, Spain: Grijalbo, 1988.

Index